LEARN TO SPEAK
UKRAINIAN
(WITHOUT EVEN TRYING)

Stephen Hernandez

Learn to speak Spanish (without even trying)

Really helpful tips on how to learn to speak Spanish it is money very well spent.

★★★★★

(Kindle Customer)

Learn to speak German (without even trying)

Learn to speak German is a super addition to this series of books from an author whose love of languages shines through in his writing.

★★★★★

(Amazon Reader)

Learn to speak French (without even trying)

5 Star!

★★★★★

(Amazon Reader)

Learn to speak Portuguese (without even trying)

5 out of 5 stars!

★★★★★

(Amazon Reader)

Learn to speak Dutch (without even trying)

So impressed by the author's infectious desire to learn and spread the joy of learning a new language

(Amazon Reader)

Learn to speak Norwegian (without even trying)

(Amazon Reader)

Learn to speak Swedish (without even trying)

(Amazon Reader)

Learn to speak Danish (without even trying)

Another great addition to this superb series of language speaking skills

★ ★ ★ ★ ★

(Amazon Reader)

To see a friend no road is too long.

A new language is a new life.

—PERSIAN PROVERB

CONTENTS

LEARNING UKRAINIAN

The purpose of this book is to teach you *how to learn*, rather than what to learn. It would be impossible to discuss the Ukrainian language's complete grammatical structure and, every Ukrainian word and its correct pronunciation in one book and if ever such a book were written it would be incredibly tedious.

The aim of this book is to *get you speaking* Ukrainian to the extent you can hold a reasonable conversation with a native speaker and you can read and understand a newspaper and magazine article written in Ukrainian. Once you have progressed that far you will not need the help of any book, course, or teacher—you will just need to practice.

Make no mistake—learning a language when you are not living in a country where it is spoken is very difficult. Not only do you not have situations where you can practice your new found learning but you are constantly bombarded by your native language as soon as you leave the classroom or your chosen place of learning. In many ways it becomes a case of perseverance. I liken it to the starting of a new exercise regime. You enroll in a local gym (giving you the added incentive that you are actually paying to get fitter). At first you are full of enthusiasm and energy so you set yourself unrealistic goals. Instead of starting off walking and progressing to running, you start off at a mad sprint and quickly tire. The novelty soon wears off and going to the gym becomes an irksome duty. Then excuses for not going begin to kick in, and before you know it you have given up altogether.

- Absolutely anyone can learn Ukrainian.
- I'm completely serious.

It doesn't matter what your excuse is. Maybe you think you stink at languages. Maybe you think you're too lazy. Maybe you flunked out of high school modern languages or maybe you just can't pronounce foreign words no matter how hard you try.

If you really want to learn Ukrainian, **you can do it.** Best of all you can do it without even trying. The only effort you have to make is to read this book (and even then you can skip the bits you don't like), make a concrete plan to study (one you can stick to), keep it fun (extremely important), and stay motivated over the long haul (self-explanatory).

- Decide on a simple, attainable goal to start with so that you don't feel overwhelmed.
- Make learning Ukrainian a lifestyle change.

- Invite Ukrainian into your daily life. That way, your brain will consider it something useful and worth caring about.
- Let technology help you out. The internet is absolutely great for learning Ukrainian—use it.
- Think about learning Ukrainian as a gateway to new experiences. Think of the fun things you want to do and turn them into language-learning opportunities.
- Make new friends. Interacting in Ukrainian is key—it will teach you to intuitively express your thoughts, instead of mentally translating each sentence before you say it. If you are a bit shy about getting the ball rolling with native speakers nearby, you can do this online (there is a whole chapter on this).
- Most of all do not worry about making mistakes. One of the most common barriers to conversing in a new language is the fear of making mistakes. But native speakers are like doting parents: any attempt from you to communicate in their language is objective proof that you are some sort of gifted genius. They'll appreciate your effort and even help you. The more you speak, the closer you'll get to the elusive ideal of "native fluency."

To start off with don't set yourself unrealistic goals or a grandiose study plan. Keep it simple. Set aside a small amount of time that you can reasonably spare even if it just means getting up 15 minutes earlier in the morning. If you set that time aside and avoid distractions that 15 minutes will be invaluable. Above all make it as fun as possible. No one said learning a new language was easy but neither should it be irksome.

You can use this book in tandem with any other learning resource you may be using at the moment if that resource is working for you. At some point, though, you will find you have your particular way of learning, and discovering that is very important. Once you find what works, you will have achieved an important milestone, and your learning will accelerate accordingly. I hope that with this book you will find your "way" sooner rather than later. That is what I designed it to do.

This book has no strict order (you can jump to and from chapters if you want), no particular rules to follow, and I definitely do not take anything for granted except the fact that you want to learn to speak Ukrainian and most probably want the experience to be as painless as possible.

I want to make it clear once again (as it is important), that this book is not designed to "teach" you Ukrainian. It is designed to help you learn how to teach yourself to speak Ukrainian with the least effort possible—hence, the sub-title: "without even trying." It gives you a process and pointers on how to learn Ukrainian effectively and easily. Consider it an autodidactic guide.

It is also a guide to learning subconsciously. By subconsciously, I do not mean that you go to sleep listening to tapes in Ukrainian or practice some kind of self-hypnosis. What we are aiming at is picking up Ukrainian without forcing the issue. The greatest aim in learning any language is being able to think in that language and not be aware that you are doing it. Then, you speak automatically without over thinking the process. Stick with me and you will obtain that goal.

Sounds impossible? It won't be by the time you have finished this book.

A journey of a thousand miles begins with a single step.

Yeah, we've all heard that one from a thousand language teachers.

As far as advice goes, that saying is about as useful as an ashtray on a motorbike.

Think about it. If you're stranded in a foreign wilderness with no idea about *how* to get where you want to go, you'll have an extraordinarily difficult time getting there no matter how many footsteps you take. In fact, you'll probably end up going around in circles.

But if you've got a map and compass, as well as some decent navigating skills, you're likely to be on your way a lot faster.

In the same way, when you're starting to learn a new language, it helps to have a road map to both guide you along and guarantee that you're still headed in the right direction when you get stuck or feel lost.

Just like physical maps, a map for language learning should be based on what other people have seen. There are a number of polyglots and dedicated language learners out there who have become cartographers of the linguistic frontier. We will be drawing on their collective experience.

We will take this collective language learning experience, along with some scientific and technical know-how, and set out on the path to learning a new language in double time.

Here are some basic strategies to get you started:

- Become your own coach—develop goals and strategies. If you have heard of bullet journals, now is a good time to put one into practice. If this fails to ring the smallest of bells in the lockers of your memory, Google it and decide if you like the idea—it comes in very handy when learning a new language.

- A lot of the time, when we start something new, we make vague statements like, "I want to be able to speak well as quickly as possible," or, "I'm going to study Ukrainian as much as I possibly can." This can be a problem because, when we create such vague goals, it can be very difficult to achieve any sort of meaningful result. That's why orienting your Ukrainian learning odyssey should start with the use of two techniques: **SMART goals** and **metacognitive strategies.**

- **SMART,** in this case, is an acronym that means Specific, Measurable, Achievable, Results, Time-bound. The synopsis of this is that you need to make really, really concrete goals that can be achieved (even if you're incredibly lazy—see next chapter). Setting realistic goals like this is an essential skill for anyone studying by themselves, as well as anyone who wishes to maximize their study time.

- **Metacognitive strategies** involves three steps. First, you plan. Ask yourself what your specific goals are and what strategies you're going to use to achieve them. Second, start learning and keep track of how well you do every day. Are you having problems that need new solutions? Write that down. Are you consistently succeeding or failing in a certain area? Keep track of that, too. And the third and final step, after a few weeks to a month, it is time to **evaluate yourself**. Were you able to achieve your goals? If not, why? What strategies did and didn't work? Then the whole process repeats again.

These two techniques naturally fit together quite well, and they're both indispensable for making sure you're cooking with gas every time you sit or lie down to study.

Total immersion (i.e., living in the Ukraine) and speaking, seeing, hearing, reading and writing it all the time is, of course, the ultimate way to learn and is certainly the ultimate goal to strive for. Most of us aren't free to move from country to country as we please and must make decisions about when the best time would be for us to go to that oh-so-wonderful country we've been daydreaming about for countless hours. So, this book is aimed mainly at people who are studying from home in their native country, but also has a large travel section for before you travel

.

The Internet

Throughout this book, I'll suggest links to websites worth visiting for more information. I assume that their content is legal and correct, but I have no way of knowing, and accept no responsibility for them. Site owners change the content all the time, web pages get deleted and sites close down in the blink of an eye. If you find an inappropriate or dead link, let me know. You'll find my e-mail address at the end of the book.

Enjoy yourself.

Languages can be difficult to master. Even the easiest of languages for English speakers can take six hundred hours to conquer, according to the Foreign Service Institute, and perhaps much more than that if you want to do something with it professionally. This is not something you can do day in, day out without getting some pleasure out of the whole *ordeal*.

Thankfully, language is as human an obstacle as it gets and is naturally tied to amazing and fulfilling rewards. Think about how wonderful it is or could be to read your favorite Ukrainian author in the original, or understand a Ukrainian film without having to look at the sub-titles, or most amazing of all, hold a conversation with someone in their native language! Language is the thing that connects us to other people and the social benefits are extremely powerful.

Just think about how often you check Facebook. Why are social networking sites so popular? Because any information connected to other people is inherently seductive. So, from the get-go, make sure that you use your language skills for what they were made for—socializing.

Sometimes, when your schedule is crazy, you'll be tempted to jettison the "fun" things that made you attracted to learning Ukrainian in the first place to get some regular practice in. Maybe you'll skip your favorite Ukrainian TV show because you can't understand it without subtitles yet (more on this later), or you'll forget to keep up with the latest news on your favorite Ukrainian singer or band.

Make time for the things that got you started. They're what motivate you and push you through when language learning seems like a brutal punishment.

Really, it's all about balance. The steps are all here, laid out for you.

Only by starting out on the journey will you gain intuitive control, the sense of masterful dexterity like that of a professional athlete or a samurai warrior.

You have your map.

Now you just need to take those first steps ...

CHAPTER ONE

LEARNING AT HOME
(even if you're really lazy)

Do you have hopes and dreams of speaking a language fluently, but you're too lazy to study?

So do many people, but they give up before they've even started because it just seems like so much effort towards an intangible goal. And seriously—who *wants* to study?

But what if I told you that your laziness, far from being a limitation, could actually make you great at learning Ukrainian?

Read on (if you can be bothered) to find out why the lazy way is often the best way and learn ways you can leverage your laziness to learn a language effectively at home.

Lazy people find better ways to do things

If you were a builder at the end of the 19th century, life was hard. Long hours. Bad pay. Little regard for health and safety. If you were really unlucky, it could even cost you your life: five men died during the construction of the Empire State

Building, and 27 died working on the Brooklyn Bridge. Mortality rates amongst builders in Victorian Britain were even more horrendous. In short, being a builder was a dangerous job.

What qualities did builders need in such a demanding and dangerous job?

Tenacity? Diligence? Stamina?

No. Not at all.

In 1868, a young construction worker named Frank Gilbreth, while observing colleagues to understand why some bricklayers were more effective than others, made a startling discovery.

The best builders weren't those who tried the hardest. The men Gilbreth learned the most from were the laziest ones.

Laying bricks requires repeating the same skilled movements over and over again: the fewer motions, the better. In an attempt to conserve energy, the "lazy" builders had found ways to lay bricks with a minimum number of motions. In short, they'd found more effective ways to get the job done.

But what do lazy bricklayers have to do with learning Ukrainian, apart from the fact that I worked as one for a while? (I wasn't very good at laying bricks, but I was excellent at being lazy!)

Well, inspired by his lazy colleagues, Gilbreth went on to pioneer "time and motion study," a technique that streamlines work systems and is still used today in many fields to increase productivity. You know that person in the operating room who passes scalpels to the surgeon and wipes their brow? Gilbreth came up with that idea.

Hiring someone to pass you things from 20 centimeters away and wipe the sweat off your own forehead? It doesn't get much lazier than that. Yet it helps surgeons work more efficiently and probably saves lives in the process.

The bottom line? The lazy way is usually the smartest way.

Over the years, Gilbreth's ideas have been attributed to people like Bill Gates, who is (falsely) reported to have said: "I will always choose a lazy person to do a difficult job because he will find an easy way to do it." (This attribution, although factually incorrect, makes a nice motivational poster to hang in your office.)

The lazy way

One of the most embarrassing episodes in my life (and there are quite a few, believe me!) was when I unadvisedly went to a parents' evening at my young daughter's primary school. The teacher asked each child in turn what their fathers did for a living. My daughter's response: "He lies on the sofa with his hands down his trousers."

Actually, that is partly true, although you may be relieved to know that I don't spend *all* my time with my hands down my trousers. If there's one thing I love more than writing, listening to the radio, and browsing the web, it's sitting or lying on the sofa in my pants, reading or watching TV—a lot of the time in foreign languages. Fortunately, with regards to writing this book, these activities aren't mutually exclusive, so I'm always on the lookout for ways to combine my favorite pastimes.

I've scoured the web to find the best resources to learn Ukrainian, and this book contains my findings. Hopefully, the information contained herein will save you a lot of time and money spent on useless systems and pointless exercises and will repay your faith in me. When you speak Ukrainian (which you will), please remember to recommend it to your friends. Even if you don't use a computer, there is enough basic information here to get you started on your path to learning Ukrainian. But I would strongly advise getting on the internet if you intend to learn from home with some degree of success.

If your school was anything like mine, you may have some experience learning languages with the "try harder" approach: page after page of grammar exercises, long vocabulary lists, listening exercises about stationary or some other excruciatingly boring topic. And if you still can't speak the language after all that effort? Well, you should try harder.

But what if there's a better way to learn a language? A lazier way, that you can use to learn a language at home and, with less effort?

A way to learn by doing things you actually enjoy? A way to learn by having a laugh with native speakers? A way to learn without taking your pajamas off?

There is.

Don't get me wrong. Languages take time and effort; there's no getting around that. This isn't about being idle.

It's about finding effective ways to learn (remember: SMART and metacognitive strategies?) so you can stop wasting time and energy on stuff that doesn't work. With that in mind, I've put together a collection of lazy (but highly effective) ways to learn a language at home or away.

They'll help you:

- Speak a language better by studying less!
- Go against "traditional" language learning methods to get better results.
- Get fluent in a language while sitting around in your undies and drinking beer (this isn't compulsory).

Don't study (much).

A lot of people try to learn a language by "studying." They try really hard to memorize grammar rules and vocabulary in the hope that one day, all the pieces will come together and they'll magically start speaking the language.

Sorry, but languages don't work that way.

Trying to speak a language by doing grammar exercises is like trying to make bread by reading cookbooks. Sure, you'll pick up some tips, but you'll never learn how to bake unless you're willing to get your hands dirty.

Languages are a learn-by-doing kind of a deal. The best way to learn to speak, understand, read, and write a language is by practicing speaking, listening, reading, and writing. That doesn't mean you should never study grammar or vocabulary. It helps to get an idea of how the language works. But if you dedicate a disproportionate amount of time to that stuff, it'll clutter your learning experience and hold you back from actually speaking Ukrainian.

You'll learn much faster by *using the language.*

Now, if you're totally new to language learning, you may be wondering how you can start using a language you don't know yet. If you're learning completely from scratch, a good textbook can help you pick up the basics. But avoid ones that teach lots of grammar rules without showing you how to use them in real life. The best textbooks are the ones that give you lots of example conversations and introduce grammar in bite-size pieces.

As soon as you can, aim to get lots of exposure to the Ukrainian language being used in a real way. If you're a lower-level learner, you can start by reading books that have been simplified for your level (called graded readers). Look for ones accompanied by audio so you can work on your listening at the same time.

If you can, keep a diary or journal of your experience with different methods of learning. Bullet journals are great for this. Never heard of them? They are basically a sort of a cross between a diary and a to-do list. Keeping one will help you see what works for you and what doesn't, and also to chart your progress.

You can buy readymade ones to suit you or design your own. You can use it for motivation when you feel like you are getting nowhere, as you will see at a glance all the progress you have made. Believe me, you will be surprised at how far you have come and sometimes you just need a little reminder to give you that motivational push.

You will also be able to see what areas you need to improve in and the types of things you are best at. When you are feeling low, go back to the stuff you are best at.

Consider how a child has learned to speak a language. Presumably, unless it was a precocious genius, it did not start off by reading a primer in grammar. Children start off by observing and identifying. Naming and pronunciation comes from hearing the description of the object from others, usually adults, or other kids fluent in the language.

Before we start off on our journey in learning to speak Ukrainian let's take a quick look at the language's background.

Ukrainian

Ukrainian is an Eastern Slavonic language spoken mainly in Ukraine. In 2016 there were about 30 million speakers of Ukrainian in Ukraine, where it is an official language. There were about 1.1 million Ukrainian speakers in Russia in 2010, and smaller numbers in other countries, particularly in Brazil (500,000), the USA (152,000), Germany (141,000), Italy (120,000) and Moldova (107,000). It is estimated that there are 40 million Ukrainian speakers worldwide.

Ukrainian is closely related to Belarusian and Russian, and is to some extent mutually intelligible with them, especially with Belarusian.

History of Ukrainian

The recorded history of the Ukrainian language began in 988, when the principality of Kyiv / Kiev (*Київ*) was converted to Christianity. Ukrainian religious material, including translations of the Bible, was written in Old Slavonic, the language used by missionaries to spread Christianity to the Slavic peoples.

In the 13th century, Ukraine became part of the Grand Duchy of Lithuanian and Ruthenian, an ancestor of Belarusian and Ukrainian became the main language. The remaining parts of Ukraine were taken over by Poland during the 16th century and Latin and Polish were used for official purposes. Ruthenian began to split into Ukrainian and Belarusian during this period.

The Cossacks later moved into eastern Ukraine and during the 17th century, their leader, Bohdan Khmelnytsky, invited Russia to help against Polish domination in 1648. During the reign of Catherine the Great, the Cossacks moved to the eastern frontiers of Russia, but Ukraine remained under Russian domination, and the Russians considered the Ukrainian language as little more than a dialect of Russian.

A decree in 1876 banned the printing or importing of Ukrainian books. Inspite of this, there was a revival of Ukrainian poetry and historiography during the 19th century.

Ukraine enjoyed a brief period of independence from 1918 to 1919, then was taken over by the USSR and declared a Soviet Republic. During the Soviet era, Russian was the main language of education and employment and Ukrainian was sidelined.

Ukraine declared independence in 1991. Since then many Ukrainian émigrés have returned to Ukraine, particularly from central Asia and Siberia.

Note, the capital of Ukraine is written Київ (Kyiv) in Ukrainian, and Киев (Kiev) in Russian. It is usually written Kiev in English, however since 1995 the Ukrainian government has written it Kyiv in legislative and official acts, and this spelling is used by international organizations such as the UN, and international news sources, such as the BBC.

Ukrainian alphabet

Learning the Ukrainian alphabet is very important because its structure is used in every day conversation. Without it, you will not be able to say words properly even if you know how to write those words. The better you pronounce a letter in a word, the more understood you will be in speaking the Ukrainian language.

Ukrainian letters are often transcribed in slightly different variations and I have tried to include a variety throughout the book so you can get used to seeing these variations. It, however, makes no difference whatsoever to their pronunciation.

Below is a table showing the Ukrainian alphabet and how it is pronounced in English, and finally examples of how those letters would sound if you place them in a word.

Ukrainian Alphabet	English Sound	Pronunciation example
А а	/a/	as in **car**
Б б	/b/	as in **best**
В b	/w/a/	as in **well**
Г г	/h/	as in **good**
Ґ г	/g/	as in **give**
Д д	/d/ /di/	as in **day**

Е е	/ɛ/	as in **Jerry**
Є є	/jɛ/ or /ⁱɛ/	as in **yellow**
Ж ж	/ʒ/	as in **pleasure**
З з	/z/ /zʲ/	as in **zodiac**
И и	/ɪ/	as in **ink**
I i	/i/ /ʲi/	as in **see**
Ї ї	/ji/	as in **yield**
Й й	/j/	as in **yours**
К к	/k/	as in **kid**
Л л	/l/, /lʲ/	as in **love**
М м	/m/	as in **man**
Н н	/n/, /nʲ/	as in **nice**
О о	/ɔ/	as in **opera**
П п	/p/	as in **pool**
Р р	/r/ /rʲ/	as in **rise**
С с	/s/ /sʲ/	as in **sing**
Т т	/t/ /tʲ/	as in **time**
У у	/u/	as in **cool**
Ф ф	/f/	as in **free**
Х х	/x/	as in the Spanish 'j' in **Jose**
Ц ц	/t͡s/, /t͡sʲ/	as in **hats**
Ч ч	/t͡ʃ/	as in **church**
Ш ш	/ʃ/	as in **shine**
Щ щ	/ʃt͡ʃ/	as in **share**
Ь ь	/◌ʲ/	indicate the softness of consonants
Ю ю	/ju/ or /ʲu/	as in **you**
Я я	/jɑ/ or /ʲɑ/	as in **yah, yahoo**

Post-it Notes

There is something you can do right now, right this minute. Start off by naming in Ukrainian the objects that surround you, write the Ukrainian name for the object on a Post-it Note, and stick it on the object. You can find the Ukrainian translation for any household object online or in a two-way dictionary. I would advise using an online dictionary if you can, as these usually include a guide to pronunciation that you can actually listen to without trying to do it phonetically.

Put the Post-it Note at eye level or some place you will encounter it immediately upon looking at the object. Begin by saying the objects name out loud—,or perhaps, if you have company, in your head. At this point, don't worry too much if your friends and family think you have gone a little crazy. You are learning a new language; they are not. Give yourself a pat on the back instead.

Below is a short list of some common things around the house to give you a start and the idea behind this method. Remember to write the name of the object in **Ukrainian** only. Preferably, put your Post-it Note on an immovable object (your spouse or significant other might take exception to having a Post-it Note stuck on their forehead, and so might your dog or cat).

Put the Post-it Notes on everything in your house (use a two-way dictionary). It is a great way to learn nouns (the name of things). Soon you will begin to identify these objects in Ukrainian without consciously thinking about it.

Household Post-it Notes:

English	Ukrainian	Pronunciation
Wastepaper basket	Корзина для паперів	Korzina dlya papyeriv
Blanket	Ковдра	Kovdra
Pillow	Подушка	Podooshka
Sheet	Простирадло	Prostiradlo
Bedspread	Покривало	Pokrivalo
Hanger (clothes)	Вішалка	Vishalka
Painting	Живопис	zivopis
House plant	Домашня рослина	Domashnya roslina
Curtains	Штори	Shtori
Rug	Килим	Kilim
Clock	Годинник	Guodinnik
Keys	Ключі	Klyochi
Toilet	Туалет	Tooalyet
Mirror	Дзеркало	Dzyerkalo
Sink	Раковина	Rakovina
Bathtub	Ванна	Vanna
Shower	Душ	Doosh
Shower curtain	Шторка для душу	Shtorka dlya dooshoo
Toilet paper	Туалетний папір	Tooalyetniy papir
Towel	Рушник	Rooshnik
Scale (bath)	Ваги	Vagui
Hair dryer	Фен	Fyen
Refrigerator	Холодильник	Kholodilʲnik
Stove	Плита	Plita

Oven	Піч	Pich
Microwave	Мікрохвильовка	Mikrokhvilʲovka
Dishwasher	Посудомийна машина	Posoodomiyna mashina
Toaster	Тостер	Tostyer
Blender	Блендер	Blyendyer
Coffee maker	Кавоварка	Kavovarka
Can opener	Відкривачка	Vidkrivachka
Pot	Горщик	Guorshtik
Pan	Каструля	Kastroolya
Frying pan	Пательня	Patyelʲnya
Kettle	Чайник	Chaynik
Mixer	Міксер	Miksyer
Trash can	Смітник	Smitnik
Spoon	Ложка	Loƶka
Knife	Ніж	Niƶ
Fork	Виделка	Vidyelka
Glass	Склянка	Sklyanka
Plate	Тарілка	Tarilka
Saucer	Блюдце	Blyodtzye
Cup	Чашка	Chashka
Bowl	Чаша	Chasha
Napkin	Серветка	Syervyetka
Pitcher	Глечик	Gulyechik
Tablecloth	Скатертина	Skatyertina
Salt shaker	Сільничка	Silʲnichka
Pepper shaker	Перечниця	Pyeryechnitzya
Sugar bowl	Цукорниця	Tzookornitzya

Write down a few useful key phrases on your cards as well. Take your pick from these:

Ukrainian key phrases:

Привіт! *(pry-vIt)* — Hello!

Вітаю! *(vi-tA-ju)* — Greetings!

Доброго ранку! *(dO-bro-ho rAn-ku)* — Good morning!

Доброго дня! *(dO-bro-ho dnja)* — Good afternoon!

Доброго вечора! *(dO-bro-ho vE-cho-ra)* — Good evening!

Як ся маєш? *(jak sjA mA-jesh)* — How are you doing?

Як справи? *(jak sprA-vy)* — How are you?

Добре, дякую! *(dO-bre, djA-ku-ju)* — I'm fine, thanks!

А в тебе? *(a v tE-be)* — And you?

Не дуже *(ne dU-zhe)* — So-so.

Дозвольте представитися *(do-zvOl'-te pred-stA-vy-ty-sja)* — Let me introduce myself.

Мене звати… *(me-nE zvA-ty)* — My name is…

Як тебе звати? *(jak te-bE zvA-ty)* — What is your name?

Радий познайомитися! *(rA-dyj po-zna-jO-my-ty-sja)* — Nice to meet you!

Звідки ти? *(zvI-dky tY)* — Where are you from?

Я з... *(ja z...)* — I'm from...

Скільки тобі років? *(skIL'-ky to-bI rO-kiv)* — How old are you?

Мені 25 років *(me-nI 25 rO-kiv)* — I am 25.

Де ти живеш? *(dE tY zhy-vEsh)* — Where do you live?

Ukrainian Articles

You may not have learned this at school, but in English the word "the" is called a definite article. That is because the word "the" points to a very specific thing. For example, you may tell someone, "I want the book," assuming that they will bring you the book you have in mind. An indefinite article refers to a thing without being specific like "a" or "an" for example: "I want a book."

The English definite article "the" does not exist in Ukrainian. Like most Slavic languages, Ukrainian does not have either definite or indefinite articles. Unlike English, a noun on its own can be considered definite without the need for a specific word to show this.

Learning the Ukrainian Articles (below) is vital to the language. Ukrainian articles are words that combine with a noun to indicate the type of reference being made by the noun. Generally articles specify the grammatical definiteness of the noun. Examples are "the, a, and an". Here are some examples:

English Articles	Ukrainian Articles
articles	artikli - артиклі
the	
a	
one	odin - один
some	dejaki - деякі
few	kiljka - кілька
the book	kniga - книга
the books	knigi - книги
a book	kniga - книга
one book	odna kniga - одна книга
some books	dejaki knigi - деякі книги
few books	kiljka knig - кілька книг

Below is a list of vocabulary for food where you can use the Definite and Indefinite Articles in Ukrainian. I find food items are some of the easiest words to assimilate and memorize, maybe because they are universal and ever-present. It is one of the reasons I use the repetition of certain words throughout the book (hammering home the vocabulary, if you like). Try to practice but also memorizing this table will help you add very useful and important words to your Ukrainian vocabulary:

English	Ukrainian
Food	ïzha - їжа
almonds	migdalj - мигдаль
bread	hlib - хліб
breakfast	snidanok - сніданок
butter	vershkove maslo - вершкове масло
candy	cukerka - цукерка
cheese	sir - сир
chicken	kurka - курка
cumin	kmin - кмин
dessert	desert - десерт
dinner	obid - обід
fish	riba - риба
fruit	frukti - фрукти
ice cream	morozivo - морозиво
lamb	jagnja - ягня
lemon	limon - лимон
lunch	obid - обід
meal	ïzha - їжа
meat	m'jaso - м'ясо
oven	pich - піч
pepper	perecj - перець
plants	roslin - рослин
pork	svinina - свинина
salad	salat - салат
salt	silj - сіль
sandwich	buterbrod - бутерброд
sausage	kovbasa - ковбаса
soup	sup - суп

sugar	cukor - цукор
supper	vecherja - вечеря
turkey	indichka - індичка
apple	jabluko - яблуко
banana	banan - банан
oranges	apeljsini - апельсини
peaches	persiki - персики
peanut	arahis - арахіс
pears	grushi - груші
pineapple	ananas - ананас
grapes	vinograd - виноград
strawberries	polunici - полуниці
vegetables	ovochi - овочі
carrot	morkva - морква
corn	kukurudza - кукурудза
cucumber	ogirok - огірок
garlic	chasnik - часник
lettuce	salat-latuk - салат-латук
olives	olivki - оливки
onions	cibulja - цибуля
peppers	perci - перці
potatoes	kartoplja - картопля
pumpkin	garbuz - гарбуз
beans	kvasolja - квасоля
tomatoes	pomidori - помідори

Sit around in your undies (just like The Naked Trader!)

Next, you'll need to practice speaking. Luckily, you can now do this on Skype, so you only need to get dressed from the waist up.

The best place for online conversation classes is italki (italki.com) Here, you can book one-on-one conversation lessons with native speakers called community tutors.

Talking to native speakers

This is, by far, the best way to learn a foreign language, but there's one problem with this method that no one talks about. To start with, those native speakers everyone is going on about may not want to talk to you.

When you start speaking a foreign language, it's all mind blanks, silly mistakes, and sounding like a two-year-old, which makes communication slow and awkward.

It's not you that's the problem. You have to go through that stage if you want to speak a foreign language.

But you need the right people to practice with. Supportive ones who encourage you to speak and don't make you feel embarrassed when you get stuck or make mistakes.

The best place to find these people?

The internet.

The fastest (and most enjoyable way) to learn a language is with regular, one-on-one speaking practice. Online tutors are perfect because it's so easy to work with them—you can do a lesson whenever it suits you and from wherever you have an internet connection, which makes it simple to stick to regular lessons.

Let's just run through how to sign up with italki, although the procedure is much the same with other online sites:

- Go to italki.com.
- Fill in your details, including which language you're learning.
- Once you get to the main italki screen, you'll see your profile with your upcoming lessons. At the moment, it says zero, so let's go ahead and set one up.
- Click on "find a teacher."
- Here, you'll find filters like "price," "availability," and "specialties." Set these to fit in with your budget, schedule, and learning goals.
- Explore the teacher profiles and watch the introduction videos to find a teacher you'll enjoy working with.
- Click on "book now," and you'll see their lesson offers.

Informal tutoring

When choosing your lessons, you'll often see "informal tutoring," which is a pure-conversation class. This kind of lesson is great value because the tutor doesn't have to prepare anything beforehand. They just join you on Skype and start chatting

Booking your first lesson

Once you've chosen the kind of lesson you'd like, choose the time that suits you, and voilà, you've just booked your first lesson with an online tutor! Well done—I know it can feel a little intimidating at first, but creating opportunities to practice is the most important thing you can do if you want to learn to speak Ukrainian. Remember: practice, practice, practice. Have I stressed that enough?

The difference between professional tutors and community tutors

When choosing a teacher, you'll also see a filter called "teacher type" and the option to choose between professional teachers and community tutors. What's the difference?

Professional teachers are qualified teachers vetted by italki—they have to upload their teaching certificate to gain this title. These classes tend to be more like "classic language lessons." The teacher will take you through a structured course, preparing lessons beforehand and teaching you new grammar and vocabulary during each lesson.

Good for:
- If you're a total beginner.
- You're not sure where to start, and you'd like guidance from an expert.

Community tutors are native speakers who offer informal tutoring, where the focus is 100% on conversation skills. They'll give you their undivided attention for an hour while you try to speak, and they'll help by giving you words and corrections you need to get your point across.

Good for:

- If you've already spent some time learning the theory and you feel like you're going round in circles. You need to put it into practice. (Remember!)
- You're happy to take control of your own learning by suggesting topics and activities you'd like to try.
- You're on a budget—these classes are usually very good value.

If both of these options are out of your budget range, you can also use italki to find a language partner, which is free—you find a native speaker of the language you're learning (in this case, Ukrainian, of course!) who also wants to learn your native language, and you teach each other. (You will find a lot of Ukrainian speakers who want and are very willing to practice their English, believe me. You can also use your social media connections, that's what it's there for—socializing! Haven't got any Ukrainian-speaking friends on Facebook? Make some.)

Important tip for finding the right tutor

Experiment with a few different tutors until you find one you click with. When you find a tutor you get along well with, they end up becoming like a friend—you'll look forward to meeting up with them online and you will be motivated to keep on showing up for your lessons.

Prepare for your first lesson

Spending a little time preparing will allow you to focus during the lesson and get as much out of it as possible. These little gems of Ukrainian can also be used to open a conversation with a native Ukrainian speaker in any real-life situation, not just chatting online

Learn the basic pleasantries

"Hello," "goodbye," "please," "sorry," and "thank you" will take you a long way!

Learn basic communication phrases

It's important to try and speak in the language as much as possible without switching back into English. Those moments when you're scrambling for words and it feels like your brain's exploding—that's when you learn the most!

Basic Ukrainian Words

Note: Don't worry if you have already seen some of these words, **repetition** is key to learning new languages and it never hurts.

| English | Ukrainian | Pronunciation |

Hi	Привіт!	Prīvit!
Good morning!	Доброго ранку!	Dobrogo ranku!
Good afternoon!	Доброго дня!	Dobrogo dniā!
Good evening!	Добрий вечір!	Dobrīī vechir!
Welcome! (greeting someone)	Ласкаво просимо!	Laskavo prosīmo!
Hello my friend!	Здоров був, друже мій!	Zdorov buv, druzhe miī!
How are you? (informal)	Як ти поживаєш?	Ak tī pozhīvaєsh?
How are you? (formal)	Як ви поживаєте?	IĀk vī pozhīvaєte?
I'm fine, thank you!	У мене все гаразд, дякую!	U mene vse garazd, diākuiū!
And you? (informal)	А ти?	A tī?
And you? (formal)	А ви?	A vī?
Good	Добре	Dobre
Not so good	Не так добре	Ne tak dobre
Long time no see	Довго не бачились	Dovgo ne bachīlīs'
I missed you (masculine)	Я сумував за тобою	IĀ sumuvav za toboiū
I missed you (feminine)	Я сумувала за тобою	IĀ sumuvala za toboiū
What's new?	Що нового?	Shcho novogo?
Nothing new	Нічого нового	Nichogo novogo
	Hvad hedder du?	Ved hell-er do?
My name is...	Mit navn er...	Meet now-n air..

Where are you from?	Hvor kommer du fra?	Vor kom-ah do fra?
I'm from...	Jeg er fra...	Jai air fra..
Entrance	Indang	In-gang
Exit	Udgang	Ool-gang
Open	Åben	Oben
Closed	Lukket	Lou-ket
Prohibited	Forbudt	For-boot
Police	Politi	Po-lee-tee
Hospital	Hospitalet	Haws-pee-tai-let
Post Office	Posthus	Post-who
City Centre	Centrum	Cen-trum
What time is it?	Hvad er klokken?	Ved air claw-gen
Toilet (Mens)	Toilet (Herrer)	Toy-let (Hair-ah)
Toilet (Womens)	Toilet (Damer)	Toy-let (Day-mah)
Merry Christmas	Glædelig Jul	Gley-thlee yool

CHAPER TWO

LEARNING UKRAINIAN ON YOUR OWN

If you want to learn Ukrainian independently, you're going to need a few things in your head-locker.

- Motivation (to keep going)
- Focus/Mindfulness (to be effective)
- Time/Patience (for everything to sink in)

Without these three things, it's impossible to learn a language.

There seems to be one killer rule to set yourself up for success: **keep it simple!**

With tonnes of language-learning websites, apps, and courses out there, it can be tempting to jump from one to the next.

But there's one golden rule to remember...

It's usually more effective to calmly work your way through one book or stick with one study method than to try different things out of curiosity. It is therefore doubly important to pick the right study methods. The best will

be referred to in this book so you don't waste your valuable study time.

The focus you'll get from this keeps self-doubt away and helps you learn more deeply.

If you are learning by yourself, for whatever reasons, you will have to *work* a little bit every day at your Ukrainian to succeed. Dedicating a regular amount of time every day, no matter how little, is more productive than learning sporadically in large chunks.

You will need to spend a lot of your time listening to Ukrainian. If you don't, how do you expect to ever be able to follow along in a conversation?

If you are completely new to studying and like to read, then there is a pretty neat way of starting off your Ukrainian adventure without depending on fixed study times.

Learn-Ukrainian (https://www.loecsen.com/en/learn-ukrainian) is a free online course in Ukrainian for beginners.

In their blurb they say: "We have adopted an objective and efficient approach to *learn how to speak* a language easily and quickly."

They suggest you do it to start with by: "Memorizing **words, phrases and practical expressions** that you can use in everyday life and that will be useful when traveling. Getting used to **pronounce** words out loud, numbers for instance, is an easy *exercise* that you can practice often and at anytime throughout the day. It will help you to get used to the sounds of your chosen language and thus make it **more familiar**. And once your holidays have begun, in Kyiv or elsewhere, you will be surprised how familiar and easy to **understand** it will seem. Furthermore, using a printed pocket *dictionary* or one on your mobile phone is always useful, particularly during a trip. It enables you to find the *translation* of new words and enrich your **vocabulary**."

It may not do all of those things but as a quick introduction to Ukrainian it is pretty good, plus its free! It's also a good platform for getting a head start on the language if you are planning a weekend in the Ukraine.

Self-study and online learning are the most flexible ways to learn anything as you can base your learning around your lifestyle rather than working to the schedule of a rigid language school. By being able to work on your Ukrainian in your lunch break, on your commute, in a cafe, or at home, you have the flexibility to learn at your own speed, making it much easier to be successful.

CHAPTER THREE

PRACTICING UKRAINIAN ON YOUR OWN

It is very important to regularly practice the Ukrainian you have learned even if it is just talking out loud to yourself. To really succeed in Ukrainian (become fluent), it is essential to practice with a native speaker, but until you have found someone to practice with, here are some ways to practice by yourself.

Think in Ukrainian

One of the main things about learning to speak a language is that you always have to learn to think in the language.

If you're always thinking in English when you speak Ukrainian, you need to translate everything in your head while you speak. That's not easy and takes time.

It doesn't matter how fluent your Ukrainian is; it's always hard to switch between two languages in your mind.

That's why you need to start thinking in Ukrainian as well as speaking it. You can do this during your daily life.

If you discover a new word in Ukrainian, reach for your Ukrainian dictionary rather than your Ukrainian-to-English dictionary. (Don't have dictionaries?—Buy some. You will need them; they can be your best friends while learning Ukrainian.) It may seem old fashioned to use printed material for looking things up nowadays (and not 'googling' it on your mobile), but the act of looking up words and writing them down imprints them on your mind and pays dividends in the long run.

Think out loud

Now that you're already thinking in Ukrainian—why don't you think out loud?

Talking to yourself whenever you're on your own is a great way to improve your language-speaking skills.

When you're reading books in Ukrainian, try doing it out loud, too.

The problem with speaking on your own is when you make mistakes. There's nobody there to correct you.

However, it's helpful to improve your ability to speak out loud, even if you make the occasional error.

Talk to the mirror

Stand in front of a mirror and talk in Ukrainian.

You could pick a topic to talk about and time yourself.

Can you talk about soccer for two minutes? Can you explain what happened in the news today for three minutes?

While you're talking, you need to watch the movements of your mouth and body.

Don't allow yourself to stop. If you can't remember the particular word, then you need to express the same thing with different words.

After a couple of minutes, it's time to look up any words you didn't know. This will allow you to discover which words and topics you need to work to improve.

Fluency over grammar

The most important thing when speaking isn't grammar; **it's fluency**.

You don't want to be stopping and starting all the time. You need to be able to have free-flowing conversations with native speakers.

Don't allow yourself to stop and stumble over phrases. A minor error here and there doesn't matter.

You need to make yourself understood rather than focus on everything being perfect.

Try some Ukrainian (tongue-twisters)

скоромовки is the Ukrainian word for tongue-twister. This includes words or phrases that are difficult to say at speed. Try out these Ukrainian tongue-twisters:

Сів шпак на шпаківню, заспівав шпак півню: "Ти не вмієш так, як я, - так, як ти, не вмію я!"

Approximate translation (literal):

A starling sat on the starling-house and sang to the rooster: "You cannot sing like I do, I cannot sing like you do!"

Драбина з повиламуваними щаблями.

Approximate translation (literal):

A ladder with broken steps.

Бавились в брудній баюрі два бобри брунатно-бурі. "Правда добре, друже бобре?" "Дуже добре, брате бобре!"

Approximate translation (literal):

Two grey-brown beavers were fooling in a mudhole. "Isn't it good, my friend?" "Very good, my brother!"

Бурі бобри брід перебрели забули бобри забрати торби.

Approximate translation (literal):

Fulvous beavers waded a ford but they forgot to take their bag (with them).

Фарбував фазан фіалки, брав фломастер у фіалки.

Approximate translation (literal):

A pheasant drew curtains and took a felt-tip from a violet.

Черепаха часто чхала, чапля чаєм частувала.

Approximate translation (literal):

A turtle repeatedly sneezed, a heron entertained (the turtle) with a cup of tea.

Яків ягідки якісь якось із галяви ніс.

Approximate translation (literal):

Yakiv once carried some berries from a glade.

Хитру сороку спіймати морока, А на сорок сорок — сорок морок.

Approximate translation (literal):

There is a trouble catching a magpie, but forty magpies mean forty troubles.

If you can master tongue-twisters in Ukrainian, you'll find that you'll improve your overall ability to pronounce challenging words in Ukrainian.

Listen and repeat over and over

Check out Ukrainian-language TV shows or movies to improve your Ukrainian (there is a chapter dedicated to this later on).

Listen carefully and, then pause and repeat. You can attempt to replicate the accent of the person on the screen.

If you need some help to understand the meaning, turn on subtitles for extra help. If you come across a word you don't recognize, you can look it up in your Ukrainian dictionary. I have already mentioned how good this is for your language learning.

Learn some Ukrainian songs

If you want a really fun way to learn a language, you can learn the lyrics to your favorite songs.

You can start with children's song and work yourself up to the classics.

And if you want a greater challenge, check out the Ukrainian rappers. If you can keep up the pace with some of these hip-hop artists, you're doing great!

Learn phrases and common sayings

Instead of concentrating on learning new words—why not try to learn phrases and common sayings?

You can boost your vocabulary and learn how to arrange the words in a sentence like a native speaker.

You need to look out for how native speakers express stuff. You can learn a lot from listening to others.

Imagine different scenarios

Sometimes, you can imagine different scenarios in which you have to talk about different kinds of things.

For example, you can pretend to be in an interview for a job in a Ukrainian-speaking country.

You can answer questions such as: "What are your biggest weaknesses?" and "Why do you want to work for us?"

When you have already prepared for such circumstances, you'll know what to say when the time comes.

Change the language on your devices

Consider changing your phone, computer, tablet, Facebook page, and anything else with a language option to Ukrainian. This is an easy way to practice Ukrainian since you'll see more of the vocabulary on a daily basis.

For example, every time you look at your phone, you'll see the date in Ukrainian, reinforcing the days of the week and months of the year. Facebook will ask you if you would like to "додати друга" *dodaty druha* ("add friend"), teaching you the verb that means "to add" - "додати."

Seeing a few of the same words over and over again will help the language feel more natural to you, and you'll find it becomes easier to incorporate them into everyday life with very little effort involved!

Research in Ukrainian

How many times a day do you Google something that you're curious about? If you use Wikipedia a few times a week, go for the Ukrainian version of the website first. Next time you need information about your favorite celebrity, look at their page in Ukrainian and see how much you can understand before switching the language to English.

Pick up a Ukrainian newspaper

You can read Ukrainian newspapers online. I recommend Експрес (Expres) (https://expres.online/) but there are plenty of choices to suit your taste. You can also download apps and read the news on your phone. You can read the articles out loud to practice Ukrainian pronunciation in addition to reading skills. This is also a great way to stay informed about what is happening in the Ukraine and the world, and helps if you get in a Ukrainian conversation.

Play games in Ukrainian

Once your phone is in Ukrainian, many of your games will appear in Ukrainian, too. Trivia games force you to be quick on your feet as you practice Ukrainian, as many of them are timed. If that isn't for you, WordBrain 2 offers an interesting vocabulary challenge in Ukrainian! (See the chapter on apps).

Watch TV Shows and You Tube videos

Don't knock Ukrainian soap operas until you try them! If you follow any British soaps, you will enjoy them. Netflix, Hulu, Amazon and Apple now offer shows and movies in Ukrainian, some of which include English subtitles so you can check how much you understand. You can also watch your favorite movies with Ukrainian subtitles.

Don't have Netflix, Hulu, Amazon or Apple? Try watching on YouTube or downloading straight from the Net. You can also check out free Ukrainian lessons on YouTube in your spare time.

This is a good way to judge the stage your Ukrainian learning has reached. If you are a beginner, look for lessons that teach you how to say the letters and sounds of the Ukrainian alphabet. It will help with your pronunciation. (See the chapter on best Ukrainian TV shows).

Get Ukrainian-language music for your daily commute

Why not practice Ukrainian during your commute? Singing along to songs will help your pronunciation and help you begin to think in Ukrainian (not a good idea if you use public transportation unless, of course, you have a superb singing voice). Try to learn the lyrics.

You can get music in any genre in Ukrainian on YouTube, just like in English. In case you haven't heard already, the Ukraine has a strong music scene which – especially over the past few years – keeps getting bigger, with upcoming Ukrainian artists rocking the national and international music scene.

Океан Ельзи (Okean Elzy - Elza's Ocean)

Is the most famous and the most decorated Ukrainian rock band in CIS (Commonwealth of Independent States). Each year Океан Ельзи plays for nearly one million people in major CEE (Central and Eastern Europe) countries.

5'nizza (pronounced "PYAT-ni-tsa" — Russian/Ukrainian for **"Friday"**)

Were an acoustic music duo from Kharkiv, Ukraine, consisting of Serhiy Babkin (Сергей Бабкин) (guitar) and Andriy Zaporozhets (SunSay) (vocals). Their music is a combination of soul, hip-hop and reggae performed using mostly acoustic guitar, sung or rapped vocals and human beatbox.

Flëur

Was an ethereal/dream pop band from Odessa, Ukraine. They were active from 2000 to 2017.

Бумбокс (Boombox)

Is a Ukrainian funky-groove band. Founded in 2004 in Kyiv by the vocalist Andriy Hlyvnyuk & guitarist Andriy "Fly" Samoylo

Drudkh (meaning "wood" in Sanskrit)

Is an atmospheric black metal band from Kharkiv, Ukraine formed in 2002.

Сергей Бабкин (Sergey Babkin)

Is a singer-songwriter from 5'nizza (see above). He was born on November 7, 1978 in the city of Kharkiv.

SunSay

Ukrainian band formed by Andrey "Sun" Zaporozhets, another ex-5'nizza member.

Esthetic Education

Esthetic Education was founded in 2004 in Kyiv, Ukraine by Louis Franck, a Belgian filmmaker and photographer living in London.

Крихітка Цахес

Is a Ukrainian pop-rock, soft-rock band formed in 1999 in Kyiv, Ukraine.

Nokturnal Mortum

Is a black/folk metal band from Kharkiv, Ukraine formed in 1994.

Ундервуд

Is a pop rock band from Crimea named after the Underwood typewriter. It was formed by two doctors from Simferopol.

Друга Ріка (Druha Rika - "Second River" in Ukranian)

Is an Ukranian rock band formed in 1996 in Zhytomyr, Ukraine.

Тартак

Is a popular rapcore, punk rock and hip-hop crossover band from Ukraine.

Hate Forest

Hate Forest was a black metal band from Ukraine that was active beginning 1995 until 2005.

Скай (Skai)

Is a Ukrainian pop-rock band founded in 2001. Singing songs both in Ukrainian and English.

Люk (Lyuk)

Are a electro-funk-lounge band from Kharkiv, Ukraine.

Gogol Bordello

Combining elements of punk, gypsy music, and Brechtian cabaret, Gogol Bordello tells the story of New York's immigrant diaspora.

You can hear most of these on the Spotify Channel. Take your pick!

Listen to podcasts in Ukrainian

While you're sitting at your desk, driving in your car on your way to work, or cooking dinner at home, put on a podcast in Ukrainian. It could be one aimed at teaching Ukrainian or a Ukrainian-language podcast on another topic.

For learning conversational Ukrainian, try Coffee Break Ukrainian, (https://coffeebreaklanguages.com/category/one-minute-ukrainian), which focuses on conversations for traveling abroad, like how to order coffee. All in one minute slices—the time it takes to drink an espresso! If you are a true beginner, Ukrainian 101 is another great one (https://www.101languages.net/ukrainian). They have all levels of Ukrainian for any student!

Duolingo (https://www.duolingo.com/course/uk/en/Learn-Ukrainian) has also just added a great new feature called "stories": fun, simple tales for learners with interactive translations and mini comprehension quizzes.

CHAPTER FOUR

A GUIDE FOR THE COMPLETE BEGINNER

If you are a complete beginner, you can consider using this book as a guide on *how* to learn and *what* to learn to enable you to speak Ukrainian as painlessly as possible. This guide will hand over the keys to learning Ukrainian for any and all potential learners, but in particular, it is for those who think they might face more trouble than most. It'll be more than enough to get you up and running.

These are the main subjects we will be covering as you begin to learn *how to learn* Ukrainian. You will probably notice that I repeat the idea of motivation throughout this book. That is because it is important! It is one of the main reasons people fail to achieve their goal of speaking a new language and give up before they really get started:

- **Motivation:** Defining your overarching goal
- **Step by Step:** Setting achievable short-term goals

- **Getting There:** Efficient Ukrainian learning resources for beginners
- **Fun:** Having fun as you learn
- **Ongoing Motivation:** Staying motivated as you learn

We will go over each of these subjects in more detail later, but for now, below is a brief overview.

Definition of Motivation: a reason or reasons for acting or behaving in a particular way.

Motivation is critical for learning a language. Good, motivating reasons for learning Ukrainian include:

- "I want to understand people at Ukrainian events."
- "I want to flirt with that cute Ukrainian at work."
- "I want to read Yuri Andrukhovych in the original."
- "I want to understand people at my local Slavic delicatessen."
- "I want to enjoy Ukrainian soap operas or TV series."
- "I need Ukrainian for work so that I can communicate with prospective clients."
- "I want to be able to make myself understood when I'm on holiday in the Ukraine."

These are all great reasons for learning Ukrainian because they include **personal, compelling motivations** that'll keep you coming back when the going gets rough.

They also guide you to **specific, achievable goals** for study (more on this later), like focusing on reading or on the vocabulary used in conversations on the dance floor.

Here are a few bad—but rather common—reasons for studying Ukrainian:

- "I want to tell people I speak Ukrainian."
- "I want to have Ukrainian on my CV."
- "I want to look smart."

Why are these bad?:

These are very likely not going to be truly motivating reasons when you can't seem to find time to open that workbook. They also don't give you any concrete desire to pay careful attention to, for example, a new tense that you've come across and how it might allow you to express yourself better.

If looking smart is your honest reason for wanting to learn a language, perhaps you could just lie and say you speak something like Quechua, which few people are going to be able to call you out on. (If you are interested, Quechua was the ancient language of the Incas and is still spoken in remote parts of South America).

Learning a language is a serious commitment

It is rarely possible to learn a language without a genuine motivation for some sort of authentic communication. That does not mean it should be painful or boring. Throughout this book, I will outline methods that make learning Ukrainian fun and interesting. When you are interested in something and having fun you do not have to consciously **TRY**, and strangely, this is when you perform at your best. You are in the *zone,* as they say.

Step by Step: Setting achievable, short-term goals.
As in life, once you are clear about your overall motivation(s), these should then be translated into achievable, short-term goals.

You're not going to immediately get every joke passed around a Ukrainian gathering and be able to respond in kind, but you should be able to more quickly arrive at goals like:

- "I'm going to place my favorite restaurant order in perfect Ukrainian." We go over this in the chapter entitled "Navigating the restaurant."
- "I'm going to memorize *and use* three words of Ukrainian slang." We go over this in the chapter entitled "Partying in Ukrainian."

I cannot stress enough the importance of correct pronunciation, as this will form the basis of your learning experience. There are a lot of free online pronunciation guides, make the most of them. It is also a good idea, if you have the equipment to record yourself and compare it to the native speaker.

If you want to take it a step further, there are some very good audio books in Ukrainian published by Languages Direct they have a whole load of books and audio books specifically designed to improve listening comprehension. The books are graded for difficulty so that you can assess your progress with each book.

Talk when you read or write in Ukrainian. *Writing* itself is an important part of language learning so read out loud (paying careful attention to pronunciation) and write in Ukrainian as much as you can. Just like when you took notes at school, writing serves to reinforce your learning.

- Watch movies with subtitles. Imitate some of the characters if you want.
- Listen to Ukrainian music, learn the lyrics of your favorite songs, and sing along with them in Ukrainian, of course.
- Join a local Ukrainian group. You'd be surprised how many there are and how helpful they can be for new language learners. This will give you a chance to practice your Ukrainian with a native speaker in a friendly and helpful environment.

CHAPTER FIVE

FLUENCY

What is fluency? Every person has a different answer to that question. The term is imprecise, and it means a little less every time someone writes another book, article, or spam email with a title like "U can B fluent in 7 days!"

A lot of people are under the impression that to be fluent in another language means to speak it as well as, or almost as well as, your native language. These people define fluency as knowing a language *perfectly*—lexically, grammatically and even phonetically. If that is the case, then I very much doubt that there are that many fluent English speakers out there. By that, I mean that they know every aspect of English grammar and know every word in the English language.

I prefer to define it as "being able to speak and write quickly or easily in a given language." It comes from the Latin word *fluentum,* meaning "to flow."

There is also a difference between translating and interpreting, though they are often confused. The easiest way to remember the difference is that translating deals with the written word while interpreting deals with the spoken word. I suppose, to be pedantic, one should be fluent in both forms, but for most people, when they think of fluency, they mean the spoken word. Nobody has ever asked me to write them something in Spanish, for instance, but I am quite often asked to say something in Spanish, as though this somehow proves my fluency—which is a bit weird when you think about it as it is only people who have no knowledge of Spanish whatsoever who ask me that and I could say any old nonsense and they would believe it was Spanish.

The next question most people ask is: how long does it take to be fluent? It is different for every person. But let's use an example to make a baseline calculation. To estimate the time you'll need, you need to consider your fluency goals, the language(s) you already know, the language you're learning, and your daily time constraints.

One language is not any more difficult to learn than another; it just depends on how difficult it is for *you* to learn. For example, Japanese may be difficult to learn for many English speakers for the same reason that English is difficult for many Japanese speakers; there are very few words and grammar concepts that overlap, plus an entirely different alphabet. In contrast, an English speaker learning French has much less work to do. English vocabulary is 28% French and 28% Latin, so as soon as an English speaker learns French pronunciation, they already know thousands of words. If you want to check the approximate difficulty of learning a new language for an English speaker, you can check with the US Foreign Service Institute, which grades them by "class hours needed to learn."

CHAPTER SIX

FORGETTING

We struggle to reach any degree of fluency because there is so much to remember. The rulebook of the language game is too long. We go to classes that discuss the rulebook, and we run drills about one rule or another, but we never get to play the game (actually put our new found language to use). On the off chance that we ever reach the end of a rulebook, we've forgotten most of the beginning already. Moreover, we've ignored the *other* book (the vocabulary book), which is full of thousands upon thousands of words that are just as hard to remember as the rules.

Forgetting is the greatest foe, so we need a plan to defeat it. What's the classic Ukrainian-language-learning success story? A guy moves to the Ukraine, falls in love with a Ukrainian girl, and spends every waking hour practicing the language until he is fluent within the year. This is the immersion experience, and it defeats forgetting with brute force. In large part, the proud, Ukrainian-speaking hero is successful because he never had any time to forget. Every day, he swims in an ocean of Ukrainian; how could he forget what he has learned?

Immersion is a wonderful experience, but if you have a steady job, a dog, a family, or a bank account in need of refilling, you can't readily drop everything and devote *that* much of your life to learning a language. We need a more practical way to get the right information into our heads and prevent it from leaking out of our ears.

I'm going to show you how to stop forgetting so you can get to the actual game. The important thing to know is what to remember so that once you start playing the game, you're good at it. Along the way, you will rewire your ears to hear new sounds and rewire your tongue to master a new accent.

You will investigate the makeup of words, how grammar assembles those words into thoughts, and how to make those thoughts come out of your mouth without needing to waste time translating.

You'll learn to make the most of your limited time, investigating which words to learn first, how to use mnemonics to memorize abstract concepts faster, and how to improve your reading, writing, listening, and speaking skills as quickly and effectively as possible.

It is just as important to understand how to use these tools as it is to understand *why* they work. Language learning is one of the most intensely personal journeys you can ever undertake. You are going into your own mind and altering the way you think.

- Make memories more memorable.

- Maximize laziness.
- Don't review. Recall.
- Rewrite the past.

How to remember a Ukrainian word forever

You can consider this part of the book to be a miniature mental time machine. It will take you back to the time when you learned as a child does.

Kids have amazing brains. They can pick up two languages in early childhood just as easily as they can learn one. Early childhood also seems to be the key period when musical training makes it much easier to acquire the skill known as perfect or absolute pitch. And that's not all: kids and teens can learn certain skills and abilities much more quickly than most adults. In a way, it makes sense that the young brain is so "plastic," or able to be molded. When we're young and learning how to navigate the world, we need to be able to acquire skills and knowledge fast.

As we age, we lose much of that plasticity. Our brains and personalities become more "set," and certain things are harder to learn or change. As adults in the rapidly changing modern world, where the ability to learn a new skill is perhaps more essential than ever, it's easy to be jealous of how quickly kids can pick up on things.

How does one go from being a baby, whose linguistic skills end with smiling, burping, and biting, to being a fluent speaker whose English is marked by appropriate diction, golden grammar, and a killer accent?

Normal, everyday children do this in about 20 months.

This brings us back to the question: how do children learn a language? And what lessons can foreign-language learners get from these precious children?

So, we're going to trace a baby's journey from babbling newborn to kindergartner. Along the way, we'll note the milestones of language development

Pre-birth

We used to think that language learning began at the moment of birth. But scientists in Washington, Stockholm, and Helsinki discovered that fetuses are actually listening inside the womb.

They gave mothers a recording of made-up words to play during the final weeks of pregnancy. The babies heard the pseudo-words around 50—71 times while inside their mother's womb. After they were born, these babies were tested. By hooking them up to an EEG, scientists were able to see images of the babies' brains when the made-up words were played.

To their astonishment, the babies remembered and recognized the words that were presented when they were in the womb.

You know what this suggests, right?
It points to prenatal language learning.

It turns out, the first day of learning language isn't when one is born, but 30 weeks into the pregnancy when babies start to develop their hearing ability. So, be careful what you say around a pregnant woman, ok? Somebody's listening.

0—6 Months

Newborn babies are keen listeners in their environments. They particularly like to listen to the voice of their mother, and they quickly differentiate it from other voices. They also learn to recognize the sounds of her language from a foreign one.

Baby communication centers on expressing pain and pleasure. And if you listen very carefully, you'll notice that babies have different types of cries for different needs. A cry for milk is different from a cry for a new diaper—although a flustered first-time father might not hear any difference.

Around the fourth month, babies engage in "vocal play" and babble unintelligible sounds—including those that begin with the letters M, P, and B. (This is when mommy swears that she heard baby say, "Mama.")

6—12 Months.

This is the peek-a-boo stage. Babies pay attention and smile when you call them by name. They also start responding to "Hi!" and "Good morning."

At this stage, babies continue babbling and having fun with language. But this time, their unintelligible expressions have put on a certain kind of sophistication. They seem to be putting words together. You could've sworn she was telling you something.

It will actually be around this time when babies learn their first words ("no," "mama," "dada," and so on).

By the 12th month, you'll have that nagging feeling that she understands more than she lets on. And you will be right. Babies, although they can't speak much, recognize a lot. They begin to recognize keywords like "cup," "ball," "dog," and "car."

And on her first birthday, she'll definitely learn what the word "cake" means.

1—2 Years Old.

This is the "Where's-your-nose?" stage.

Babies learn to differentiate and point to the different parts of their bodies. They're also very receptive to queries like "Where's Daddy?" and requests like "Clap your hands" or "Give me the book."

As always, her comprehension goes ahead of her ability to speak. But in this stage, she'll be learning even more words. Her utterances will graduate into word pairs like "eat cake," "more play," and "no ball."

This is also the time when she loves hearing those sing-along songs and rhymes. And guess what? She'll never tire of these, so be prepared to listen to her favorite rhymes over and over and over again.

2—4 Years Old.

There will be a tremendous increase in learned words at this stage. She now seems to have a name for everything—from the cups she uses to her shoes and toys. She gains more nouns, verbs, and adjectives in her linguistic arsenal.

Her language structure becomes more and more complicated. Her sentences get longer, and her grammar mistakes get slowly weeded out. This time, she can express statements like "I'm hungry, Mommy" or "My friend gave me this."

She'll start to get really talkative and ask questions like, "Where are we going, Daddy?"

By this time, you'll begin to suspect that she's preparing to ask ever more difficult questions.

The child has learned the language and has become a native speaker.

So, what are the lessons we can take away from children as foreign-language learners?

We've just gone over how babies progress to acquire their first language. Is there something in this process that adult language learners can emulate in their quest to learn foreign languages?

Well, as it turns out, there is.

Understanding this early childhood learning process has major implications for adult language learners.

In this chapter, we're going to peek behind the curtain and look even deeper into how children learn languages to reap four vital lessons.

Each one of these lessons is an essential part of linguistic success.

1. The Centrality of Listening.

We learned in the previous section that listening comes very early in the language-acquisition process. Babies get a masterclass on the different tones, rhythms and sounds of a language even before they see the light of day.

Without listening, they'd have no building blocks from which to build their own repertoire of sounds.

Listening is so important for language acquisition that babies don't fully develop their language capabilities without the ability to hear. Thus, we have the deaf-mute pairing. How can one learn to speak when one can't even hear others or oneself doing it?

In addition, children who suffer hearing problems early in life experience delays in their expressive and receptive communication skills. Their vocabulary develops slower, and they often have difficulty understanding abstract words (e.g., extreme, eager, and pointless). Their sentences are also shorter and simpler.

In general, the greater the hearing loss, the poorer the children do in academic evaluations.

Listening is central to language.

It's the first language skill humans develop.

And yet, how many language programs pound on the issue of listening as a central skill, as opposed to grammar or vocabulary?

Listening is deceptive, isn't it? It seems like nothing's happening. It's too passive an activity, unlike speaking. When speaking, you actually hear what was learned. The benefits of listening are initially unheard (pun intended).

Contrary to common belief, listening can be an intensely active activity.

So, as a foreign-language learner, you need to devote time to actively listening to your target language. Don't just play those podcasts passively in the background. Actively engage in the material. If at all possible, don't multitask. Sit down and don't move—like a baby who hasn't learned how to walk. Take every opportunity to listen to the language as spoken by native speakers. When you watch a movie or a language learning video, for example, don't just focus on the visual stimulation. Listen for the inflections, tones, and rhythms of words.

It may not look like much, but, yes, listening is that powerful.

2. The Primacy of Making Mistakes

Listening to a one-year-old talk is such a delight. They're so cute and innocent. Their initial statements betray a string of misappropriated vocabulary, fuzzy logic, and grammar violations.

When a 1-year-old points to a dog and says, "Meow," we find it so cute. When his older sister says, "I goed there today," we don't condemn the child. Instead, we correct her by gently saying, "No, Sally, not goed. Went!"

We aren't as kind to adults. We're even worse to ourselves.

Ever since we learned in school that making mistakes means lower test scores, we've dreaded making them. Mistakes? Bad.

And we carry over this fear when we're learning a foreign language as adults.

That's why, unless we're 100% sure of its correctness, we don't want to blurt out a single sentence in our target language. First, we make sure that the words are in their proper order and that the verbs are in the proper tense and agree with the subject in number and gender.

Now, something tells me that a ten-month-old has no problems committing more mistakes in one sentence than she has words. In fact, she probably won't admit that there's something wrong—or ever know that something's wrong. She just goes on with her life and continues listening.

Why don't we follow this spirit of a child?

We already know that it works because the kid who once exclaimed, "My feets hurt," is now galloping towards a degree in sociology.

As a foreign-language learner, one of the things you need to make peace with is the fact that you're going to make mistakes. It comes with the territory, and you're going to have to accept that.

Make as many mistakes as you can. Make a fool out of yourself like a two-year-old and laugh along the way. Pay your dues. And if you're as diligent in correcting those mistakes as you are making them, soon enough you'll be on your way to fluency.

3. The Joy of Repetition

When your daughter is around 6-12 months old, playing peek-a-boo never gets old for her. She always registers genuine surprise every time you reveal yourself. And she'd laugh silly all day—all because of a very simple game.

And remember how, when your children were around one to two years old and they couldn't get enough of those sing-songy rhymes? They wanted you to keep pressing the "replay" button while watching their favorite cartoon musical on YouTube. You wondered when they would get sick of it.

But lo and behold, each time was like the first time. They weren't getting sick of it. In fact, it got more exciting for them.

Repetition. It's a vital element of learning. If there's one reason why babies learn so fast, it's because they learn stuff over and over—to the point of overlearning.

Adults never have the patience to overlearn a language lesson, to repeat the same lesson over and over without feeling bored to tears. Adults quickly interpret this as being "stuck". This lack of forward motion is promptly followed by the thought that time is being wasted. They think they should quickly press on to the next lesson—which they do, to the detriment of their learning.

We repeat a vocabulary word three times and expect it to stay with us for life—believing it will now be saved in our long-term memory. Quite unrealistic, isn't it?

In the prenatal experiment where made-up words were played to babies still in the womb, each word was heard by the baby at least 50 times. (Is it really a wonder, then, that the baby, when tested, recognized the words?)

Repetition is vital to learning. In fact, many apps take the concept further and introduce the idea of spaced repetition. SRS (spaced repetition software) can be an invaluable tool in your language learning toolkit. Try out Anki (https://apps.ankiweb.net/), FluentU (https://www.fluentu.com/), or SuperMemo (https://www.supermemo.com/en).

Unless you're a genius with an eidetic memory, repetition will be one of your most important allies in the quest for foreign-language mastery.

Repetition can take the form of replaying videos, rereading words, rewriting vocabulary, re-listening to podcasts, and re-doing games and exercises.

Keep on repeating until it becomes a habit. Because that's what a language ultimately is.

4. The Importance of Immersion

Immersion can actually push your brain to process information in the same way native speakers do.

And is there anything more immersive than a baby being born and experiencing the world by observation?

Think about what the baby is experiencing. She's like an Englishman suddenly being dropped in the middle of China without access to the internet.

Everything is new.

So, you use your innate abilities to make generalizations, read context, listen to native speakers, and imitate how they speak.

Everything is on the line. You've got to learn how to communicate fast; otherwise, you won't get to eat—even when you're sitting at a Chinese restaurant. It's a totally immersive experience where you're not learning a language just for kicks or for your resume. You're doing it for your very survival. (That takes care of the "motivation" part of your learning.)

There's nothing fake about a child learning a language. It's a totally immersive and authentic experience—all their early language lessons are learned in a meaningful social context. I have yet to meet a baby who learned his first language by enrolling in a class.

For the adult language learner, immersion can be experienced remotely. One way of achieving immersion is by getting exposed to as many language-learning videos as possible.

Another way is something we touched on earlier: spaced repetition.

Remember that time you crammed information for an exam?

(Don't worry, we've all been there.)

You, like many others, may have spent an all-nighter memorizing every page of your notes and trying desperately to make up for countless days you decided to hold off on studying.

While you may have performed well on the exam, think about how much you recalled a few weeks after the test date.

How much of that information did you remember? If you're like most humans, the answer is probably not very much.

Cramming does not work, especially when learning a new language.

You can try, but unfortunately, you won't get very far if you try to learn the Ukrainian subjunctive tense in one night. Now, you may wonder, "If I was able to recall information so well at the time of an exam, why has it dropped from my memory soon after?"

Well, there's science behind this! Research proves that cramming intense amounts of information into our brain in a short period is not an effective way for long-term learning.

British author H.E. Gorst mentioned in his book The Course of Education that cramming is what "produce[s] mediocrity". What he means is that cramming doesn't provide us with the ability to think critically and effectively apply our knowledge in creative ways.

Yet cramming is still becoming more and more popular among students of all ages.

If it's so ineffective, why do we cram?

Fingers point to improper time management as the number one cause. If we better prioritize our time, we can more efficiently learn new information. By cramming, we may absorb information that can be easily regurgitated the following day.
But say goodbye to that information because it's going to disappear at an exponential rate as time goes on.

Cramming trades a strong memory now for a weak memory later. Unfortunately, we sometimes cling to short-term gratifications and fail to strive for long-term benefits. Before you banish all hope for your memory, there's an alternative method to learning that may give your brain the love it needs.

In psychology, there is a theory of memorization and learning called the "spacing effect". The spacing effect is the idea that we remember and learn items more effectively when they are studied a few times over a long span of time.

So, is frequent repetition the solution? Not quite.

Since cramming is out the window, you may think it's smarter to study material over and over again. It's crucial to note that while repetition is important, not all repetition is created equally. You'll want to space out the repetitions each time you study a set of information.

But determining how long to wait in between studying can also be a tricky matter. If you practice too soon, your brain will begin passively remembering information, which will not stick over time. If you practice too late, you will have forgotten the material and have to spend extra time relearning it.

Add to this the complexity of individual learning and memorization patterns, and you have a recipe for guaranteed memory loss.

Thankfully, there is the aforementioned software available today to help us pinpoint the sweet spot of optimal learning. Just when our forgetfulness dips below a certain level, these programs jump in and keep our brains on track.

Spaced Repetition Software

Spaced repetition software (SRS) computer programs are modeled after a process similar to using flashcards. Users enter items to be memorized into the program, and they are then converted into electronic "decks" that appear on-screen in a one-by-one sequential pattern.

Usually, the user clicks one time to reveal the question or front of the generated card. A second click will reveal the answer or back of the flashcard. Upon seeing the answer, the user then indicates the difficulty of the card by telling the program how challenging it was.

Each following card's order of appearance is not random. In fact, SRS programs use algorithms to space out when each card will appear again on the screen. Cards given "easy" ratings will appear later than cards given "hard" ratings, thus allowing users to spend more time studying the cards that are more difficult. The tough ones will show up more often until they are mastered, giving you the chance to actively learn them more efficiently than with other learning styles.

Using Spaced Repetition for Language Learning

To put this into context, let's pretend you spend an evening studying a hundred Mandarin words you didn't know before. You continue studying until you've completely memorized the words. Let's say it takes you an hour to do this.

Immediately after reviewing these words, your memory of them will be quite high. However, over time, you will naturally begin forgetting the material you learned. And since it was your first time learning these words, your use-it-or-lose-it brain is more likely to ditch this new material at a faster pace. The new knowledge isn't yet considered important enough to be etched into your brain cells.

However, the second time you study the same words, it will take you less time to master the set than it did the first time. Perhaps this time it only takes you 30 minutes to memorize the hundred words. Congratulations! You've completed your first spaced repetition.

So, does this mean you'll have to keep repeating the information you want to learn for the rest of your life? Not exactly. While it does require long-term review to keep information fresh on our minds, the time spent on review becomes shorter and less frequent over time.

With each successive review, it will take you less and less time to fully recall the information. As you begin mastering a set of words, you'll find yourself whizzing through each card. Eventually, information will become so memorable that you know it by heart. This is when you know you're ready to move onto a new, more challenging deck.

Self-discipline Ultimately Trumps All

Remember, while these programs may have wonderful language-learning techniques, they won't be effective unless you have the self-discipline to use them on an ongoing basis. If you're still at a loss for where to begin with organizing your own flashcards, check out Olly Richards's "Make Words Stick", a guide for language learners just like you looking to get more out of their SRS.

Make it a habit to open up and use the software mentioned above. If you set aside some time every day to do your SRS studying, you'll see noticeable results sooner than you might imagine.

If, like me, you sometimes want to get away from the computer and get back to basics, you can make your own flashcards and use them manually. You can buy packets of blank cards at the post office or at any stationery suppliers. Write the English word on one side and the Ukrainian word on the reverse. You can choose your own words, but here are some to get you started, plus some useful phrases. Take your pick. Don't forget to include the Ukrainian pronunciation if you need it.

Ukraine	Pronunciation	English
Хто?	*khto*	Who?
Що?	*scho*	What?
Коли?	*ko-LY*	When?
Який?	*ja-kYj*	Which?
Яка? (fem.)	*ja-KA*	Which?
Де?	*de*	Where?
Як?	*jak*	How?
Чому?	*cho-mU*	Why?
Скільки?	*skIL'-ky*	How much?
Вулиця	*vU-ly-tsja*	Railway station
Пошта	*pO-shta*	Post office
Кафе	*ka-fE*	Cafe
Ресторан	*re-sto-rAn*	Restaurant

Ринок	rY-nok	Market
Супермаркет	su-per-mAr-ket	Supermarket
Музей	mu-zEj	Museum
Лікарня	li-kAr-nja	Hospital
Метро	me-trO	Metro
Автобус	av-tO-bus	Bus
Трамвай	tram-vAj	Tramway
Таксі	ta-ksI	Taxi
Де це?	dE tse	Where is it?
Це далеко?	tse da-LE-ko	Is it far from here?
Туди чи сюди?	tu-dY chy sju-dY	Is it this or that way?
В яку сторону	v jakU stO-ro-nu	Which side
Як пройти до	jak proj-tY do	How to go to
Я голодний	ja ho-LOd-nyj	I am hungry
Я хочу пити	ja khO-chu pY-ty	I am thirsty
Я візьму	ja viz'-mU	I'll take
Принесіть, будь ласка	pry-ne-sIt', bud' LAs-ka	Bring me, please
Сніданок	sni-dA-nok	Breakfast
Обід	o-bId	Lunch
Вечеря	ve-chE-rja	Dinner
Десерт	de-sErt	Dessert
Вино	vy-nO	Wine
Вода	vo-dA	Water
Сік	sik	Juice
Сир	syr	Cheese
Фрукти	frUk-ty	Fruits
Риба	rY-ba	Fish
М'ясо	mjA-so	Meat

Хліб	khlib	Bread
Сіль	sil'	Salt
Смачного!	sma-chnO-ho	Enjoy your meal!
Вам допомогти?	vam do-po-moh-tY	Do you need help?
Допоможіть мені, будь ласка	do-po-mo-zhIt' me-nI bud' LAs-ka	Help me please
Котра година?	kot-rA ho-dY-na	What time is it?
Дозвольте...	doz-vOL'-te	Allow me...
Чи можу я...?	chy mO-zhu ja	May I...?
Я вас не розумію	ja vas ne ro-zu-mI-ju	I don't understand you
Ви розумієте мене?	vy ro-zu-mI-je-te me-nE	Do you understand me?
Я не знаю	ja ne znA-ju	I don't know
Повторіть, будь ласка?	pov-to-rIt' bud' LAs-ka	Could you repeat, please?
Я заблукав	ja za-blu-kAv	I'm lost
Я не розмовляю українською	ja ne ro-zmov-ljA-ju uk-ra-jIns'-ko-ju	I don't speak Ukrainian
Що це?	scho tse	What's that
Що це означає?	scho tse o-zna-chA-je	What does it mean?
Говоріть повільніше, будь ласка?	ho-vo-rIt' po-vil'-nI-she bud' LAs-ka	Could you speak slower?
Ви говорите англійською?	vy ho-vO-ry-te anh-LIjs'-ko-ju	Do you speak English?
Як туди пройти?	jak tu-dY pro-jtY	How can I go there?
Що з вами?	scho z vA-my	Are you okay?

Ukrainian	Pronunciation	English
Що ви хочете?	*scho vy khO-che-te*	What do you want?
Скільки це коштує?	*skIL'-ky tse kOsh-tu-je*	How much does it cost?
Дякую!	*djA-ku-ju*	Thank you!
Дуже дякую!	*du-zhe djA-ku-ju*	Thank you very much!
Будь ласка!	*bud' LAs-ka*	You are welcome!
Нема за що!	*ne-mA za scho*	My pleasure!
Перепрошую...	*pe-re-prO-shu-ju*	Excuse me...
Вибачте!	*vy-bach-te*	I'm sorry! (for a mistake)
Мені шкода	*me-nI shko-dA*	I'm sorry (commiseration)
Нічого	*ni-chO-ho*	Nevermind
Не переживай	*ne pe-re-zhy-vAj*	Don't worry
Я розумію	*a ro-zu-mI-ju*	I understand
Все гаразд	*vse ha-rAzd*	It's okay
Молодець!	*mo-lo-dEts'*	Well done!
Вітаю!	*vi-tA-ju*	Congratulations!
Я кохаю тебе!	*ja ko-khA-ju te-bE*	I love you
Овва!	*Ov-va*	Wow!
На жаль...	*na zhAl'*	Unfortunately
Шкода	*shko-dA*	It's a pity
Агов!	*a-hOv*	Hey!
Хай йому грець...	*khAj jo-mU hrets'*	Damn it...
Якого дідька?	*ja-kO-ho dId'-ka*	What the hell?
Так	*tak*	Yes
Ні	*ni*	No

Можливо	*mozh-LY-vo*	Maybe
Завжди	*zav-zhdY*	Always
Ніколи	*ni-kO-ly*	Sometimes
Звичайно!	*zvy-chAj-no*	Sure!
Сьогодні	*s'o-hOd-ni*	Today
Завтра	*zAv-tra*	Tomorrow
Вчора	*vchO-ra*	Yesterday
Бувай!	*bu-vAj*	Bye!
Па-па!	*pa-pA*	See you!
До завтра!	*do zAv-tra*	See you tomorrow!
До зустрічі!	*do zU-stri-chi*	See you soon!
До побачення!	*do po-bA-chen-nja*	Goodbye!
Всього найкращого!	*vs'o-hO na-jkrA-scho-ho*	All the best!
Будьте здорові!	*bUd'-te zdo-rO-vi*	Take care!
Гарного вечора!	*hAr-no-ho vE-cho-ra*	Have a nice evening!

That should be enough to keep you going for a while!

We will be returning to childlike learning in Chapter Thirteen—"Learning Like a Child," as this lies at the heart of learning without mentally cramming.

Children are new to the learning process. They constantly see and experience things for the first time. They pause to listen to noises, try things over again until they master it, observe language until they can speak it, and ask if they don't know what something means.

As we grow, we identify other ways to efficiently gather information. However, with this, we sometimes stop paying attention to the details in our everyday lives that can provide us with fresh insight and information.

Consider these tips on how to rekindle this childlike process for obtaining knowledge.

Take Time to Observe

Start paying more attention to the things around you. Take time to appreciate the clouds in the sky. Pay attention to how your coworker's, partner's, child's day is going. Become aware of the people you are in line with at the checkout counter. Have a purpose in your observation, whether it's to better understand human nature, be more effective with your time, or gain an appreciation for others.

Go Exploring

Coming across things you have not seen or experienced before can help you appreciate things like a child would. Hike on a new trail, visit a place you've never been, or try a different route to work. Look at the things you see every day with a new eye. Consider how you would perceive them if it was the first time you'd ever noticed them.

Learn from Everyday Moments

Pause to think about the things you do every day. This can be a good practice if you feel you don't have much opportunity to learn new things or if you feel you are not progressing in your education. Assess what you have learned during your day. For instance, did a conversation not go as well as you planned? Evaluate what went well and what could have been different.

Consider how you can avoid a similar situation in the future. Write down the knowledge you have gained in a journal and review it occasionally. See where you have made improvements and how you have grown from these experiences. Note: This also helps with motivation.

Model Other People's Good Qualities

Start paying attention to the good qualities in others. Make a list of these traits and determine how you can emulate them. Work on the qualities one by one until you master them.

Take Time to Read

If you are busy, which most people are, look for ways you can incorporate reading into your schedule. Note: If you do not mind having to use a dictionary every minute, read dual-language Ukrainian books (the translation sits alongside the page you are reading).

These are a brilliant learning tool and hugely enjoyable. You will extend your vocabulary marvelously without even noticing.

Listen to audio books in your car, read on the bus, take a couple minutes of your lunch break, or put a book next to your bed where you can read a couple pages before you go to sleep. Or, to start you off, here are some Ukrainian/English parallel texts you can try online for free and if you enjoy them, purchase some:

https://www.lonweb.org/daisy/ds-ukrainian-lorna.htm

Try different genres. Ask people what their favorite books are and read them—not only will you gain more knowledge from the books, but you will learn more about those around you by understanding the books they like. Study famous and influential people and events in history. Read both fiction and nonfiction. Do some research on the life of the author. Find out what world and local events were taking place at the time the book was written.

Talk to Others

Share with others the things you are discovering, whether it's something you read in the news or heard about in another conversation. By talking about what you are learning, you can better understand and retain the knowledge you gain. It can also help you discover fresh perspectives.

Be a Hands-on Person

Find a new creative outlet. Research how to prune rose bushes and practice on the ones in your yard. Follow instructions on how to cut tile and create a mosaic table. Take something apart to ascertain how it works. Enroll in a continuing education course on NorthOrion, such as photography, ceramics, yoga, or bowling.

However you decide to do it, incorporate learning into your everyday routine. Select those methods that come naturally to you. Be willing to look at gaining knowledge as a child does, unembarrassed and optimistically. You may find that you can gain the same enthusiasm.

Please understand that when I say you should "learn like a child," I am not telling you to suddenly revert to wearing diapers and gurgling. I am talking about using some of the intuitive language learning processes that we use as children.

Adults have some advantages, which we will examine, and children have different ones. We can learn to use both precisely because we are adults.

One thing that is for sure: we don't have the same amount of time as children, so we need to optimize the time we do have to make time for language learning. But we can also utilize the time we spend doing mundane tasks to our advantage— listening to Ukrainian, for example.

The other thing you can't do is fully immerse yourself in the language (unless you are moving abroad, of course).

Your brain is nothing like a child's. The latter is a clean slate, and yours is like a graffiti-covered wall. So, when we want to learn a language, we have to clear our minds as much as possible. This is where mindfulness is so useful—more on that later.

Adults have a huge advantage insofar as first - and second - language acquisition are basically the same thing.

Adults are further advanced when it comes to cognitive development. What's more, they have already acquired their first language. It gives them the advantage of having pre-existing knowledge!

All these factors influence the cognitive structures in the brain and make the process of second-language acquisition fundamentally different from the ones occurring when you learn a mother tongue.

As an adult, you have the huge advantage over a child of being able to learn the most important grammar rules of a language when you want instead of having to acquire them slowly and through trial and error.

As I mentioned previously, adults have pre-existing language knowledge. Children have to learn the mechanics of their mother tongue, while, as adults, we have a more developed grasp of how language works. After all, almost all of us know what conjugations or adjectives are. What's more, adults are outstanding pattern-finding machines—it's much easier for us to deduce and apply language rules!

To sum up—as adults, we can learn really fast. But it all depends on how much we want to learn. Motivation is key.

Learning requires effort. We know that instinctively, and it sometimes seems that there is no way around it. The trick is to make that effort enjoyable; then it will no longer seem like an effort. It is just like someone who is happy with their job compared to someone who hates it. One will wake up in the morning looking forward to going to work, and the day will fly by; the other will dread getting up and drag themselves to work, and the day will also drag on interminably.

Your language learning experience is up to you, and as an adult, you have the ability to make it as enjoyable and as challenging as you wish. It is a mindset. Once you learn to see your mindset, you can start to choose your mindset. As with everything—you will reap what you sow.

CHAPTER SEVEN

UKRAINIAN GRAMMAR

Yes, I know, and I'm sorry, but you have to tackle it sometime if you want to master Ukrainian. Remember, if you are not interested in learning grammar (I can't blame you, although it makes things a lot easier in the long run), you can simply skip this chapter. If you prefer, skip it for now and come back to it later or learn it in bits—doable chunks. I actually recommend skipping backwards and forwards as you will find it easier the more you learn the spoken language.

If grammar really does get you down and you find it a hard slog, see the next chapter, which is on motivation.

Ukrainian grammar covers a lot of territory and I'm making a bit of an assumption that you're at least a bit familiar with English grammar because you're reading this in English. If it's your native language, you probably had some lessons about the difference between a noun and a pronoun even if it was years ago at school.

There is some good news though because many of Ukrainian grammar elements are similar to English ones.

Although, some concepts will seem completely alien, and it will take a while for you to get your head around them.

Ukrainian Grammar

Grammar is often the most feared part of learning a new language. After all, grammar has all of those rules and it can be almost impossible to memorize them all. In fact, the reason that many people feel frustrated when they are learning a new language is due to all of the grammar rules.

Instead of learning about all of the myriad Ukrainian grammar rules in the beginning, it makes sense to learn only what you need to know to start learning the actual language.

Once you have the basics down, you will find that learning and understanding all of the other grammar rules come more naturally.

Ukrainian grammar is not as difficult as some other languages might be. Learning the basics happens very quickly for most people, and it can be that way for you as well. Before long, you will understand Ukrainian grammar well enough to gain confidence when constructing your own sentences.

The Noun: Gender

The noun (іменник [i'mɛn:ɪk]) — is the main part of speech and it is the basis of Ukrainian grammar. Ukrainian nouns have three genders, they can be singular and plural and what is more important they have seven cases. Unlike English they do not have articles.

Types of cases:

1. Nominative

2. Genitive

3. Dative

4. Accusative

5. Instrumental

6. Locative

7. Vocative

Every case in Ukrainian language is named after a specific word which helps to identify the question needed to be put down to a noun, therefore children at school are taught to memorize the questions according to the names of the cases.

Nominative case (Називний відмінок): хто? що?

The nominative case is the easiest one as it answers direct questions: *who?* and *what?*

The word "називний" is derived from Ukrainian "назва" (a name), so basically it is a dictionary form of a noun, which **names** the object in the sentence:

His name is Oleh. — Його звати Олег.

If a noun is **a subject** in the sentence, it has to be nominative case:

The girl is playing the piano. — Дівчинка грає на піаніно.

If a noun is **a part of a predicate** (stays after a dash, which replaces "to be"):

He's brother is a doctor. — Його брат — лікар.

Genitive case (Родовий відмінок): кого? чого?

The genitive case shows that something or somebody is possessing or not possessing to somebody or something else.

The word "родовий" is derived from Ukrainian "рід" (a gender, a generation) and the question you can put is: whose gender?, so it's basical purpose is to point out the **possession**, belonging, membership of the object:

The girl's piano. — Піаніно дівчинки.

In some **negative** sentences:

I do not have a credit card. — У мене немає кредитної картки.

Dative case (Давальний відмінок): кому? чому?

The word "давальний" is derived from Ukrainian "давати" (to give) and the question you can put is: *to give to whom?*

He gave a candy <u>to a boy</u>. — Він дав цукерку хлопчику, or to show something to somebody, or to tell somebody something, or to explain, to present etc:

He did not tell (to) his friend that secret. — Він не розказав своєму другові той секрет.

Accusative case (Знахідний відмінок): кого? що?

The word "знахідний" is derived from Ukrainian "знаходити" (to find) and the question you can put is: *to search for whom? to search for what?*, in this case it is a direct object of a verb (action):

He is searching for mom. — Він шукає маму.

Instrumental case (Орудний відмінок): ким? чим?

This case is used when you want to express that someone or something is used by or works with somethng or somebody else.

The word "орудний" is derived from Ukrainian "орудувати" (to operate with, to handle with) and the question you can put is: *who to handle with? what to handle with?*

He paints with a brush. — Він малює пензликом.

With the preposition з(зі) (with):

Mother went to the theater with sister. — Мати пішла в театр з сестрою.

Travelling by transport or going on foot, walking along the street, city or other long distances:

I walk along this street every day. — Я гуляю цією вулицею щодня.

When somebody is interested, engaged or involved in something (somebody):

His girlfriend is interested in history. — Його подруга цікавиться історією.

Locative case (Місцевий відмінок): на кому? на чому?

This case indicates the location. This case is used **only with a preposition**.

The word "місцевий" is derived from Ukrainian "місце" (a place) and the question you can put is: *on what? on whom?* (but only the location, not the destination!).

The cat is sitting in the armchair. — У кріслі сидить кіт. (location, Locative case)

But:

The cat jumped in (into) the box. — Кіт стрибнув у коробку. (destination, Accusative case)

When telling time (with a prepositon **о** (at)):

He came at nine o'clock. — Він прийшов о дев'ятій годині.

Vocative case (Кличний відмінок)

The vocative case doesn't have any questions. It is used only in the direct speech when somebody is addressing somebody else.

"Mother, put it please on the shelf." — "Мамо, поклади це, будь ласка, на полицю."

Depending on the noun's gender, number or case the other parts of speech (i.e. adjectives, pronouns, prepositions, numerals and verbs) will change.

For example:

Цей чоловік кладе книжку на стіл. — *This man is putting (puts) a book on the table.*

What we have here is the main noun "чоловік" (a predicate) which is masculine, singular and in nominal case (answers the question: "who?"). According to this we have to change the pronoun and the verb.

Now let's talk about the genders

There are 3 of them:

1. Masculine *(чоловічий рід).*

2. Feminine *(жіночий рід).*

3. Neuter *(середній рід).*

Masculine

Nouns that are obviously 'male': чоловік — a man, хлопець — a boy, батько — a father, брат — a brother, друг — a (boy)friend, містер — Mister, бик — a bull, півень — a rooster etc.

Mostly all animals which don't have a specific gender distinction in their names: поні — pony, шимпанзе — chimpanzee, какаду — cockatoo, кенгуру — kangaroo etc.

Mostly have no endings: дуб — an oak, лоб — a forehead, зошит — a notebook, клас — a class, біль — a pain, сміх — a laughter etc.

More rarely have **-а** or **-о** endings: Микола — Mykola (Michael), дядько — an uncle, тато — dad.

Feminine

Nouns that are obviously 'female': жінка — a woman, дівчина — a girl, мати — a mother, сестра — a sister, подруга — a (girl)friend, місіс — Missis, корова — a cow, курка — a hen etc.

Mostly have **-а** or **- я** endings: голова — a head, рука — a hand, шафа — a wardrobe, стіна — a wall, земля — an earth, мрія — a dream etc.

More rarely have no endings: тінь — a shadow, ніч — a night, радість — a joy.

Neuter

Nouns that indicate animal babies and have **-а** or **- я** endings: курча — a chicken, ягня — a lamb, теля — a calf, порося — a piglet, цуценя — a puppy, кошеня — a kitten etc.

Mostly have **-о** or **-е** endings: вікно — a window, дерево — a tree, село — a village, дзеркало — a mirror, плече — a shoulder, море — a sea etc.

May also have **-я** endings: знання — a knowledge, обличчя — a face, плем'я — a tribe, ім'я — a name.

Combined

There is also a **combined** type of gender which works both for masculine and feminine, masculine and neuter, feminine and neuter or even all three of them!

These are:

Nouns that mainly have emotion value, name some creature or a specific person and point at their inherency: бідолаха — a poor thing, волоцюга — a tramp, заїка — a shutterer, ненажера — a heavy eater, слуга — a servant, сирота — an orphan, листоноша — a postman etc.

Foreign surnames, Ukrainian surnames with **-ко** or **-чук** endings: Шевченко, Петренко, Демчук, Ковальчук etc.

Some alien words, such as: директор — a principal, director, економіст — an economist, менеджер — a manager, декан — a warden, кандидат — a candidate, доцент — a docent, хірург — a surgeon, стоматолог — a dentist etc

Nouns that have **-o** ending and mean bad qualities of a person: ледащо — a lazybone, базікало — a chatterbox etc.

The Noun (cont.): Declensions

Declensions are groups of nouns gathered due to their specific endings and genders.

There are four declensions and the first and second of these declensions are also sub-divided into three different groups: hard, soft and mixed.

It works out something like this:

1. I declension
   - hard group
   - soft group
   - mixed group

2. II declension
   - hard group
   - soft group
   - mixed group

3. III declension

4. IV declension

I declension (Перша відміна)

Feminine, masculine and combined nouns with **-a(-я)** ending: суддя (a judge), стеля (a ceiling), жінка (a woman), базіка (a chatterbox), каліка (a cripple) etc.

Depending on what consonant stands before the ending there are three groups of nouns:

Group	The last consonant in the word	Example
hard	a hard consonant, except *ж, ч, ш, щ, дж*	голова (a head), рука (a hand), дорога (a road), краса (a beauty)
mixed	a hard consonant (*ж, ч, ш, щ, дж*)	вежа (a tower), миша (a mouse), площа (a suqare, a palce), круча (a steep)
soft	a soft consonant	мрія (a dream), земля (a ground), свииня (a pig), пісня (a song)

II declension (Друга відміна)

Masculine nouns with **zero** and **-о** endings: кінь (a horse), сон (a dream), рот (a mouth), батько (a father) etc.

Neuter nouns with **-о,-е,-я** endings: слово (a word), вікно (a window), горе (a grief), серце (a heart), знання (a knowledge), обличчя (a face) etc.

Depending on what consonant stands before the ending there are three groups of nouns:

Group	The last consonant in the word	Example
hard	a hard consonant, except *ж,ч, ш, щ, дж*	зу**б** (a tooth), зошит (a notebook), ді**д** (a grandfather), село (a vilage), крило (a wing)
mixed	a hard consonant (ж, ч, ш, щ, дж)	ні**ж** (a knife), чита**ч** (a reader), пле**че** (a shoulder), прізви**ще** (a surname, a second name)
soft	a soft consonant (<u>masculine nouns</u>)	учен**ь** (a student), ден**ь** (a day), біл**ь** (a pain), геро**й** (a hero), кра**й** (a land, a region)
soft	a consonant, except *ж,ч, ш, щ, дж* before **-е** ending (neuter nouns)	сон**це** (a sun), мо**ре** (a sea), сер**це** (a heart)
soft	a soft consonant before **-я** ending (<u>neuter nouns</u>)	умін**ня** (a skill), знан**ня** (a knowledge), полум'**я** (a flame), пі**р**'я (a feather)

Nouns with **-р** suffixes:

Group	Rule	Example
hard	Nouns with **-ар, -ер, -єр, -ир, -ір, -їр, -ор, -ур, -юр, -яр** suffixes; the stress does not change after declension	жар (a fever), фужер (a wine glass), кар'єр (a pit), жир (a fat), звір (an animal), Каїр (Cairo), інспектор (inspector), абажур (abatjour), бардюр (border stone), капіляр (capilar)
mixed	nouns with **-ар, -ир** suffixes; the stress switches to an ending in plural form	лікар (a doctor), воротар (a goalkeeper), секретар (a secretary), поводир (a sighted person; a guide-dog)
soft	names of people by their profession or activity with stressed **-яр** suffix	маляр (a painter), школяр (a schoolboy), каменяр (a bricklayer), газетяр (a newsagent)

III declension (Третя відміна)

Feminine nouns with **zero ending**: річ (a thing), тінь (a shadow), сіль (a salt), любов (a love) etc.

Feminie noun **мати** (a mother).

IV declension (Четверта відміна)

Neuter nouns with **-a(-я)** endings, which after declension achieve **ен-, -ат-, -ят-** suffixes: кошеня (a kitten), ягня (a lamb), плем'я (a tribe), ім'я (a name) etc.

1. *-ат-, -ят- suffixes*

теля — теляти

ягня — ягняти

порося — поросяти

курча — курчати

Such neuter nouns with *-а(-я)* endings mostly mean little animals or names of undersized things.

2. *-ен suffix*

ім'я (a name) — імені

плем'я (a tribe) — племені

сім'я (seed) — сім<u>е</u>ні (there is also a word "сім'я" which means "a family"; they may be written the same way, but they have different stresses: "сім'я" (a family) and "сім'я" (seed))

вим'я (udder) — вим<u>е</u>ні

тім'я (a krone) — тім<u>е</u>ні

These are all neuter nouns with "-ен" suffix. As you can see their special feature is an <u>apostrophe before "-я"</u> ending.

The Adjective: General information

The adjective (прикметник [prɪk'mɛtnɪk]) is a part of speech which defines the subject and answers the question: "який?" "яка?" "яке?" (**which?/what?/what kind?**) and "чий?" "чия?" (**whose?**).

The adjectives can define:

Colour: білий (white), чорний (black), блакитний (blue).

Size: великий (big), малий (small, little), широкий (wide), вузький (narrow).

Age: молодий (young), старий (old).

Flavour: солодкий (sweet), кислий (sour).

Odour: запашний, духмяний (fragrant).

Material: металевий (metal), дерев'яний (wooden), пластиковий (plastic).

Quality: твердий (hard), м'який (soft), гнучкий (flexible), рідкий (liquid).

Possession: сестрин (sister's), мамин (mom's).

Appearance: гарний (beautiful), стрункий (slim, thin).

Immanence: добрий (kind), злий (angry, evil), щирий (sincere).

Location: місцевий (local), сільський (rural), обласний (regional).

Space: далекий (far, distant), близький (near, close).

Time: ранковий (morning), пізній (late).

The adjective can be changed according to gender, number and case of the noun it defines:

солодк**ий** шоколад — sweet chocolate (singular, masculine gender, Nominative case).

солодк**а** цукерка — sweet candy (singular, feminine gender, Nominative case) солодке морозиво — sweet ice cream (singular, neuter gender, Nominative case).

солодкі яблука — sweet apples (plural, Nominative case).

The Adjective: Cases

Depending on the consonant before the ending adjectives can be divided into two groups:

1. Hard group:

The hard consonant before -ий ending: добрий (kind), червоний (red), чистий (clean), низький (short).

All the possessive adjectives: мамин (mother's), батьків (father's).

2. Soft group:

The soft consonant before -ій, синій (dark blue), ранній (early), колишній (former, ex), справж ній (true).

Adjectives with -їй ending: безкраїй (immense, endless).

3. And a special group of adjectives with -ций ending, which is a part of -лиций ("лице" means "face"): груглолиций (round-faced), блідолиций (pale-faced).

Hard group (stresses are underlined)

Case	Singular			Plural
	mascu line	**neute r**	**feminin e**	
Nominative	високий	високе	висока	високі
Genitive	високого		високої	високих
Dative	високому		високій	високим
Accusative (1)	висок-ий/ого	високе	високу	висок-і/их
Instrumental	високим		високою	високими
Locative (2)	висок-ому/ім		високій	високих

високий [wɪ'sɔkɪj] — tall, high

Soft group (stresses are underlined)

-ій ending

Case	Singular			Plural
	mascu line	**neute r**	**feminin e**	
Nominative	синій	синє	синя	сині
Genitive	синього		синьої	синіх
Dative	синьому		синій	синім
Accusative (1)	син-ій/ього	синє	синю	син-і/іх
Instrument al	синім		синьою	синіми
Locative (2)	син-ьому/ім		синій	синіх

синій ['sɪnʲij] — (dark) blue

-їй ending (stresses are underlined)

Case	Singular			Plural
	mascu line	**neute r**	**feminin e**	
Nominativ e	безкр<u>а</u>**їй**	безкр<u>а</u>є	безкр<u>а</u>я	безкр<u>аї</u>
Genitive	безкр<u>а</u>**його**		безкр<u>а</u>**йої**	безкр<u>аї</u>х
Dative	безкр<u>а</u>**йому**		безкр<u>аї</u>й	безкр<u>аї</u>м
Accusative (1)	безкр<u>а</u>-їй/**його**	безкр<u>а</u>є	безкр<u>а</u>ю	безкр<u>а</u>-ї/їх
Instrument al	безкр<u>аї</u>м		безкр<u>а</u>**йою**	безкр<u>аї</u>ми
Locative (2)	безкр<u>а</u>-йому/їм		безкр<u>аї</u>й	безкр<u>аї</u>х

безкраїй [bɛz'krajij] — immense, endless

"-лиций" adjectives (stresses are underlined)

Case	Singular			Plural
	mascu line	**neute r**	**feminin e**	
Nominative	круглол<u>и</u>-**ций**	круглол-<u>и</u>це	круглол<u>и</u>-ця	круглол<u>и</u>ці
Genitive	круглол<u>и</u>**цього**		круглол<u>и</u>-**цьої**	круглол<u>и</u>цих
Dative	круглол<u>и</u>**цьому**		круглол<u>и</u>ц-	круглол<u>и</u>цим

			ій	
Accusative (1)	круглоли ц-ий/ього	круглол- ице	круглоли- цю	круглоли ц-і/их
Instrumental	круглолиц<ins>им</ins>		круглоли- цьою	круглоли цими
Locative (2)	круглолиц-ьому/ім		круглолиц- ій	круглоли цих

1. **-ого**, **-ього** and **-их**, **-іх** endings are used with animate (as well as inanimate) nouns, while **-ий**, **-ій** and **-і** are used only with inanimate ones:

a) Вона шукає висок**ого** чоловіка. — She is searching for a tall man.

Тут немає висок**их** чоловіків. — There are no tall men here.

but you cannot say:

Тут немає високі чоловіки.

b) Мені потрібен висок**ий** стіл. — I need a high table.

Я не бачу тут високі будівлі. — I do not see high buildings here.

as well as:

Я не бачу тут високих будівель. — I do not see high buildings here.

2. **-ому, -ьому** endings are more popular (are used for both animate and inanimate nouns), while **-ім** are less (are used only for inanimate nouns):

На **синьому** столі. На **синім** столі. — On the blue table.

3. Adjectives with **-ий** ending are the most popular, while **-ій** adjectives are less popular and there are few **-їй** and **-лиций** adjectives;

4. the stress in the adjectives does not change.

The Verb

The verb (дієслово /dijɛslowo/) — is a part of speech which describes the state or action of an object. It answers the questions: що робити?/що зробити? (what to do?).

Ukrainian verb forms:

1. Infinitive.

2. Finite verbs.

3. Adjectival participle.

4. Adverbial participle.

5. Non-finite verbs.

Ukrainian verb categories:

- Aspect: perfective and imperfective.

- Transivity: transitive and intransitive verbs.

- Voice: active, passive and reflexive-middle.

- Mood: indicative, subjunctive and imperative.

- Tense: past, present and future.

- Person: first, second and third.

- Number: singular and plural.

- Gender: masculine, feminine and neuter.

Infinitive

The **infinitive** of a verb is its basic form (all verbs in the dictionary are infinitives).

Ukrainian infinitives end with a suffix **-ти (-ть)**, after which there can be used suffix **-ся**.

Example:

дума-ти (to think), чита-ти (to read), смія-ти-ся (to laugh).

As a basic form of a verb infinitive bare only some of the verb's general categories (i.e. aspect, transivity and voice). On the other hand they do not have person, number, tense, mood or gender.

In sentences infinitives can function as:

- a subject:

  Говорити правду — це чесність із собою. — Telling truth is being honest with yourself.

- a predicative:

  Розмовляти у громадському транспорті — невиховано. — Talking in public transport is impolite.

- an object:

  Він мріє поїхати до Італії. — He dreams to go to Italy.

- an adverbial:

  Вона прийшла до мене, щоб забрати свою книжку. — She came to me to take her book.

- a modifier:

Знати усе й про всіх — його обов'язок. — To know everything about everyone is his responsibility.

Finite verbs

Finite verbs in Ukrainian language can express several grammatical categories (listed above).

One verb can express almost all of them at once, for example:

Вона написала листа. — She wrote a letter.

The verb *написала* has perfective aspect, active voice, indicative mood, past tense, singular number, feminine gender and is transitive (though it does not state a specific person, as *написала* can be used with the first (I), second (you) or third (she) singular person).

Adjectival participle

Adjectival participle, or nominal form of the verb, expresses the character of an object by action. It is inflected by gender, number and cases which are the same as the noun it modifies.

In sentences they function as modifiers.

Example:

<u>Написаний</u> ним вірш не сподобався нікому. — Nobody liked the poem <u>written</u> by him.

Adverbial participle

Adverbial participle is an unchanging form of the verb that expresses an action or state as a definition of another action or state and bares qualities of both the verb and adverb.

In sentences they function as adverbials.

Example:

<u>Прийшовши</u> додому, він одразу подзвонив другові. — After he <u>came</u> back home he immediately phoned his friend.

Non-finite verbs

Non-finite verbs in Ukrainian are called *безособові* which means they do not have person. These verbs end with **-но, -то** and express action without reference to the actor. In sentences they function as independent words and are predicates in sentences with no subject.

Examples:

Тут <u>написано</u>, що завтра вихідний день. — It <u>is written</u> here that tomorrow is a day off.

Цю сукню пошито на замовлення. — This dress is tailor-made. (This dress is sewn on request.)

Preposition: Location and Destination

When telling the location of or destination to a particular object you may encounter some difficulties with what preposition to use or how to change the noun according to it.

The most popular prepositions and their common usage are as follows:

The main points of telling the location and destination:

- depending on the preposition and the question put to the sentence there can be 4 different cases involved in: Genitive, Accusative, Instrumental, Locative;

- Locative case is never involved in telling the destination, it can only point on the location of an object.

Abbreviations used in the following examples:

location — loc.

destination — dest.

Genitive — Gen.

Accusative — Acc.

Instrumental — Inst.

Locative — Loc.

Ha (on): Locative, Accusative

стіл [stʲil] — a table (masculine)

Examples using cat:

Де кіт? — **Where** is the cat?: loc.

Кіт **на столі**. — The cat is on the table.: loc., Loc.

Кіт сидить **на столі**. — The cat is sitting on the table.: loc., Loc.

Куди застрибнув кіт? — **Where** has the cat jumped?: dest.

Кіт застрибнув **на стіл**. — The cat has jumped on the table.: dest., Acc.

Куди ти кладеш кота? — **Where** are you putting a cat?: dest.

Я кладу кота **на стіл**. — I am putting a cat on the table.: dest., Acc.

Random examples:

На картині зображені міфічні істоти. — There are mythical creatures depicted in the picture. (**On the picture** are depicted mythical creatures.): loc., Loc.

Минулого літа він був **на морі**. — Last summer he was at the seaside. (Last summer he was **on the sea**.): loc., Loc.

На вулиці спекотно. — It is hot outside. (It is hot **on the street**.): loc., Loc.

На автобусній **зупинці** нікого немає. — There is nobody at the bus stop. (**On the bus stop** there is nobody.): loc., Loc.

Він вішає картину **на стіну**. — He hangs a painting **on the wall**.: dest., Acc.

Я ходжу **на роботу** щодня. — I go to work everyday. (I go **on work** everyday.): dest., Acc.

у, в (in): Locative, Accusative

коробка [kɔ'rɔbka] — a box (feminine)

Cat examples:

Де кіт? — **Where** is the cat?: loc.

Кіт **у коробці**. — The cat is in the box.: loc., Loc.

Кіт сидить **у коробці**. — The cat is sitting in the box.: loc., Loc.

Куди заліз кіт? — **Where** has the cat climbed?: dest.

Кіт заліз **у коробку**. — The cat has climbed in the box.: dest., Acc.

Куди він кладе кота? — **Where** is he putting a cat?: dest.

Він кладе кота **у коробку**. — He is putting a cat in the box.: dest., Acc.

Random examples:

Діти вивчили багато нового **у школі**. — The children learned a lot of new things at school. (The children learned a lot of new **in school**.): loc., Loc.

Він вчиться **в університеті**. — He studies at the university. (He studies **in the university**.): loc., Loc.

Наша фірма вклала багато грошей **у цю будівлю**. — Our company has invested a lot of money **in** this **building**.: dest., Acc.

Його донька сидить **вдома**, бо захворіла. — His daughter is sitting at home because she is ill. (His daughter is sitting **in home** because she is ill.): loc., Loc.

У цьому **домі** ніхто не живе. — Nobody lives **in** this **house**.: loc., Loc.

Він кидає камінці **у річку**. — He is throwing little stones **in** the **river**.: dest., Acc.

Notes

- Preposition **у** is used when the next word begins (or previous ends) with <u>a consonant</u>, while **в** is used before (or after) <u>a vowel</u>.

- "вдома" means being or staying at somebody's own house and "у домі" means being or staying in some random house.

з, зі, із (from, out): Genitive

Cat-examples:

Звідки вистрибнув кіт? — **Where** has the cat jumped **out (from)**?: dest.

Кіт вистрибнув **з коробки**. — The cat has jumped out (from) the box.: dest., Gen.

Ти дістаєш кота **з коробки**. — You are pulling a cat out of (from) the box.: dest., Gen.

Random examples:
Звідки ти? — **Where** are you **from**?: dest.

Я з Аргентини. — I am **from Argentina**.: dest., Gen.

Він приїхав **з Німеччини.** — He came **from Germany**.: dest., Gen.

Notes

- Prepositions *з, зі, із* have the same meaning. Preposition **зі** is often used when the next word begins (or previous ends) with two or more consonants, while **з** is used when the next word begins (or previous ends) with a consonant or a vowel. **із** is often used between two consonants, but is still less popular unlike **з**, which is used the most.

за (behind): Instrumental, Accusative

стіл [stʲil] — a table (masculine)

Cat-examples:

Де кіт? — **Where** is the cat?: loc.

Кіт **за столом**. — The cat is behind (at) the table.: loc., Inst.

Кіт сидить за столом. — The cat is sitting behind (at) the table.: loc., Inst.

Куди стрибнув кіт? — **Where** has the cat jumped?: dest.

Кіт стрибнув **за стіл**. — The cat jumped over the table.: dest., Acc.

Вона кладе кота **за стіл**. — She is putting a cat behind (at) the table.: dest., Acc.

Random examples:

Бабуся сидить **за столом**. — The granny is sitting **at the table**.: loc., Inst.

Вони стоять **за будинком**. — They are standing **behind the building**.: loc., Inst.

За дверима нікого немає. — There is nobody **at the door**.: loc., Inst.

Гаманець впав **за шафу**. — The wallet fell **over the wardrobe**.: dest., Acc.

перед (before, in front of): Instrumental

коробка [kɔ'rɔbka] — a box (feminine)

Cat-examples:

Де кіт? — **Where** is the cat?: loc.

Кіт **перед коробкою.** — The cat is in front of the box.: loc., Inst.

Кіт сидить **перед коробкою.** — The cat is sitting in front of the box.: loc., Inst.

Random examples:

Перед будинком зібрався натовп. — A crowd had gathered **in front of the building**.: loc., Inst.

над (above): Instrumental

стіл [stʲil] — a table (masculine)

Cat-examples:

Де кіт? — **Where** is the cat?: loc.

Кіт **над столом.** — The cat is above the table.: loc., Inst.

Кіт сидить **над столом.** — The cat is sitting above the table.: loc., Inst.

Random examples:

Над нашими **головами** пролетів літак. — The plane flew **above** our **heads**.: loc., Inst.

під (under): Instrumental, Accusative

стіл [stʲil] — a table (masculine)

Cat-examples:

Де кіт? — **Where** is the cat?: loc.

Кіт **під столом**. — The cat is **under the table**.: loc., Inst.

Кіт сидить **під столом**. — The cat is sitting **under the table**.: loc., Inst.

Куди заліз кіт? — **Where** has the cat crawled?: dest.

Кіт заліз **під стіл**. — The cat has crawled **under the table**.: dest., Acc.

Random examples:

Він спить **під** теплою **ковдрою**. — He is sleeping (sleeps) **under** the warm **blanket**.: loc., Inst

Вона сховала свій щоденник **під ліжком**. — She has hidden (hid) her diary **under the bed**.: loc., Inst.

Її сестра кладе коробку **під стіл**. — Her sister puts the box **under the table**.: dest., Acc.

між (between): Instrumental, Accusative

Cat-examples:

Де кіт? — **Where** is the cat?: loc.

Кіт **між столами**. — The cat is **between the tables**.: loc., Inst.

Кіт сидить **між столами**. — The cat is sitting **between the tables**.: loc., Inst.

Куди заліз кіт? — **Where** has the cat crawled?: dest.

Кіт заліз **між столи**. — The cat has crawled **between the tables**.: dest., Acc.

Random examples:

Між нами немає таємниць. — There are no secrets **between us**.: loc., Inst.

Вони побігли **між дерева**. — They have run **between the trees**.: loc., Acc.

біля (near, at): Genitive

стіл [stʲil] — a table (masculine)

Cat-examples:

Де кіт? — **Where** is the cat?: loc.

Кіт **біля стола**. — The cat is **near the table**.: loc., Gen.

Кіт сидить **біля стола**. — The cat is sitting **near the table**.: loc., Gen.

Random examples:

Біля будинку зібрався натовп. — The crowd gathered at the building. (**At the building** gathered the crowd.): loc., Gen.

до (to): Genitive

Cat-examples:

Куди біжить кіт? — **Where** is the cat running?: dest

Кіт біжить **до миски**. — The cat is running (runs) **to the bowl**.: dest., Gen.

Random examples:

Я йду **додому**. — I am going home. (I am going **to home**.): dest., Gen.

Він їде **до магазину** за продуктами. — He is going (by vehicle) **to the store** for groceries.: dest., Gen.

Note:

- "додому" means literally "to home" (when talking about going home), is a set phrase and written together, if you write it separately — "до дому" — it will mean going to a random home, building rather than returning to your own home.

від (from): Genitive

Cat-examples:

Звідки біжить кіт? — **Where** is the cat running **from**?: dest.

Кіт біжить **від миски**. — The cat is running (runs) **from the bowl**.: dest., Gen.

Random examples:

Від себе не втечеш. — You cannot run **from yourself**.: dest., Gen.

Ці листи **від моєї подруги**. — These letters are **from my friend**.: dest., Gen.

Ми прочитали текст **від початку і до кінця**. — We have read the text **from the beginning (and) to the end**.: dest., Gen.

Note:

- "від і до" (*lit.* 'from and to'), is a short version of a set phrase "від початку і до кінця" and is often used instead of its longer counterpart, especially in everyday speech.

- Він пояснив нам як вирішити тест **від і до**. — He explained us how to solve the test **from the begining to the end**.

Numerals: General

Numerals are devided into cardinals (cardinal numerals) and ordinals (ordinal numerals).

In turn **cardinals** are divided into:

- basic cardinals: нуль (zero), один (one), два (two), три (three), чотирнадцять (fourteen), сто десять (hundred and ten), тисяча (thousand) etc.

- fractions: одна шоста (1/6), дві сьомих (2/7), пів (half), півтора (one and a half) etc.

- assembled: двоє (two), четверо (four), п'ятеро (five) etc.

- undesignated cardinals: багато (many/much), мало (few/little), кілька (few/little) etc.

Ordinal numerals are formed by adding endings **-ий/ій, -а/я, -е/є, -і** to the corresponding cardinal numerals depending on the gender and number, which makes them look like adjectives of hard and soft groups.

For example:

дванадцять (twelve) + ий = дванадцятий (twelfth): masculine, singular;

дванадцять (12) + а = дванадцята (12th): feminine , singular;

дванадцять (12) + е = дванадцяте (12th): neuter , singular;

дванадцять (12) + і = дванадцяті (12th): plural.

Overall numerals can be:

- **simple** numerals with one radical: один (1), три (2), сто (100), перший (first);

- **complex** numerals with two or more radicals: одинадцять (11), п'ятнадцять (15);

- **composite** numerals which consist of two or more simple or complex numerals: сто двадцять (120), триста сорок (340).

Notes:

1. Cardinal numerals change according to cases but do not have genders.

Exceptions are:

one - один (masculine), одна (feminine), одне (neuter), одні (plural);

two - два (masculine, neuter), дві (feminine);

both - обидва (masculine, neuter), обидві (feminine);

one and a half - півтора (masculine, neuter), півтори (feminine).

2. Some assembled cardinals have the same translation as the basic cardinals (e.g. два, двоє — two) but are for the *most part* used with nouns portraying living beings and nouns which have only plural form.

For example:

четверо хлопців (four boys), семеро ягнят (seven lambs), троє дівчат (three girls);

восьмеро ножиць (eight scissors), троє дверей (three doors):

ножиці (scissors), двері (doors) in Ukrainian language have only plural forms.

Numerals: Basic cardinals

1 - 10

1 — один, одна, одне*

2 — два, дві**

3 — три

4 — чотири

5 — п'ять

6 — шість

7 — сім

8 — вісім

9 — дев'ять

10 — десять

*one — один (masculine), одна (feminine), одне (neuter), одні (plural);

**two — два (masculine, neuter), дві (feminine).
The rest of the cardinals do not have genders or numbers.

11 - 19

These numerals are formed by adding **-надцять** to the corresponding number of units:

11 — одинадцять (один + надцять)

12 — дванадцять (два + надцять)

13 — тринадцять (три + надцять)

14 — чотирнадцять (чотири + надцять)

15 — п'ятнадцять (п'ять + надцять)

16 — шістнадцять (шість + надцять)

17 — сімнадцять (сім + надцять)

18 — вісімнадцять (вісім + надцять)

19 — дев'ятнадцять (дев'ять + надцять)

20, 30, 40, 50, 60, 70, 80, 90

Numerals **20** and **30** are formed by adding -*дцять* to the numerals 2 and 3 respectively:

20 — двадцять (два + дцять)

30 — тридцять (три + дцять)

40 — сорок

Numerals **50**, **60**, **70**, **80** are formed by adding suffix -*десят* to the numerals 5, 6, 7, 8 respectively:

50 — п'ятдесят (п'ять + десят)

60 — шістдесят (шість + десят)

70 — сімдесят (сім + десят)

80 — вісімдесят (вісім + десят)

90 — дев'яносто

100, 1000, 1000000, 1000000000

100 — сто

1,000 — тисяча

1,000,000 — мільйон

1,000,000,000 — мільйярд

200, 300, 400, 500, 600, 700, 800, 900

200 — двісті

Numerals **300**, **400** are formed by adding suffix -*ста* to the numerals 3, 4 respectively:

300 — триста (три + ста)

400 — чотириста (чотири + ста)

Numerals **500**, **600**, **700**, **800**, **900** are formed by adding suffix -*сот* to the numerals 5, 6, 7, 8, 9 respectively:

500 — п'ятсот (п'ять + сот)

600 — шістсот (шість + сот)

700 — сімсот (сім + сот)

800 — вісімсот (вісім + сот)

900 — дев'ятсот (дев'ять + сот)

2000, 3000, 4000, 5000, 6000, 7000, 8000, 9000

2000 — дві тисячі

3000 — три тисячі

4000 — чотири тисячі

5000 — п'ять тисяч

6000 — шість тисяч

7000 — сім тисяч

8000 — вісім тисяч

9000 — дев'ять тисяч

Composite basic numerals

Composite numerals consist of two or more numerals and are written separately.

For example:

21 — двадцять один, двадцять одна, двадцять одне

22 — двадцять два, двадцять дві

23 — двадцять три

24 — двадцять чотири

...

66 — шістдесят шість

...

87 — вісімдесят сім

...

102 — сто два, сто дві

...

134 — сто тридцять чотири

...

292 — двісті дев'яносто два

...

1007 — тисяча сім

...

3584 — три тисячі п'ятсот вісімдесят чотири

...

10508 — десять тисяч п'ятсот вісім

Numerals: Ordinals

Ordinal numerals (with some exceptions) are formed by adding endings **-ий/ій**, **-а/я**, **-е/є**, **-і** to the corresponding cardinal numerals depending on the gender and number.

-ий/ій — masculine, singular;

-а/я — feminine, singular;
-е/є — neuter, singular;

-і — plural.

1 - 10

1 — перший, перша, перше, перші

2 — другий, друга, друге, другі

3 — третій, третя, третє, треті

4 — четвертий, четверта, четверте, четверті

5 — п'ятий, п'ята, п'яте, п'яті

6 — шостий, шоста, шосте, шості

7 — сьомий, сьома, сьоме, сьомі

8 — восьмий, восьма, восьме, восьмі

9 — дев'ятий, дев'ята, дев'яте, дев'яті

10 — десятий, десята, десяте, десяті

11 - 19

11 — одинадцятий, одинадцята, одинадцяте, одинадцяті

12 — дванадцят**ий/а/е/і**

13 — тринадцят**ий/а/е/і**

14 — чотирнадцят**ий/а/е/і**

15 — п'ятнадцят**ий/а/е/і**

16 — шістнадцят**ий/а/е/і**

17 — сімнадцят**ий/а/е/і**

18 — вісімнадцят**ий/а/е/і**

19 — дев'ятнадцят**ий/а/е/і**

20, 30, 40, 50, 60, 70, 80, 90

20 — двадцят**ий**, двадцят**а**, двадцят**е**, двадцят**і**

30 — тридцят**ий/а/е/і**

40 — сороков**ий/а/е/і**

50 — п'ятдесят**ий/а/е/і**

60 — шістдесят**ий/а/е/і**

70 — сімдесят**ий/а/е/і**

80 — вісімдесят**ий/а/е/і**

90 — дев'яност**ий/а/е/і**

100, 1000, 1000000, 1000000000

100 — сот**ий/а/е/і**

1,000 — тисячн**ий/а/е/і**

1,000,000 — мільйонн**ий/а/е/і**

1,000,000,000 — мільярдн**ий/а/е/і**

200, 300, 400, 500, 600, 700, 800, 900

200 — двохсот**ий/а/е/і**

300 — трьохсот**ий/а/е/і**

400 — чотирьохсот**ий/а/е/і**

500 — п'ятсот**ий/а/е/і**

600 — шістсот**ий/а/е/і**

700 — семисот**ий/а/е/і**

800 — восьмисот**ий/а/е/і**

900 — дев'ятисот**ий/а/е/і**

2000, 3000, 4000, 5000, 6000, 7000, 8000, 9000
2000 — двохтисячн**ий/а/е/і**

3000 — трьохтисячнн**ий/а/е/і**

4000 — чотирьохтисячнн**ий/а/е/і**

5000 — п'ятитисячнн**ий/а/е/і**

6000 — шеститисячнн**ий/а/е/і**

8000 — восьмитисячнн**ий/а/е/і**

9000 — дев'ятитисячнн**ий/а/е/і**

Composite ordinal numerals

Composite numerals consist of two or more numerals and are written separately. Only the last numeral is changed into ordinal, the rest are cardinals.

For example:

21 — двадцять перший, двадцять перша, двадцять перше

22 — двадцять другий, двадцять друга, двадцять друге

23 — двадцять третій, двадцять третя, двадцять третє

...

66 — шістдесят шостий/а/е/і

...

87 — вісімдесят сьомий/а/е/і

...

102 — сто другий/а/е/і

...

134 — сто тридцять четвертий/а/е/і

...

292 — двісті дев'яносто другий/а/е/і

...

1007 — тисяча сьомий/а/е/і

...

3584 — три тисячі вісімдесят четвертий/а/е/і

...

10508 — десять тисяч п'ятсот восьмий/а/е/і

Numerals: Cases
The types of declining of numerals in the Ukrainian language:

1. Declining of numeral один (one)

Numeral *один (одна, одне, одні)* is declined as pronoun *той (та, те, ті).*

Case	Singular			Plural
	masculine	neuter	feminine	
Nominative	один	одн**е**	одн**а**	одн**і**
Genitive	одн**ого**		одні**сї** (одн**ої**)	одн**их**
Dative	одн**ому**		одн**ій**	одн**им**
Accusative	один (одн**ого**)	одн**е**	одн**у**	одн**і** (одн**их**)
Instrumental	одн**им**		одні**сю** (одн**ою**)	одн**ими**
Locative	одн**ому**		одн**ій**	одн**их**

Stresses are underlined.

2. Declining of numerals два (two), три (three), чотири (four)

Case	masculine /neuter	feminine		

Nominative	два	дві	три	чотири
Genitive	дв**ох**	дв**ох**	трь**ох**	чотирь**ох**
Dative	дв**ом**	дв**ом**	трь**ом**	чотирь**ом**
Accusative	два (дв**ох**)	дві	три (трь**ох**)	чотири (чотирь**ох**)
Instrumental	дв**ома**	дв**ома**	трь**ома**	чотир**ма**
Locative	дв**ох**	дв**ох**	трь**ох**	чотирь**ох**

Stresses are underlined.

3. Declining of numerals п'ять-десять (5-10) and with -дцять, -десят

Case	7	13	50
Nominative	сім	трина**дцять**	п'ят**десят**
Genitive	сем**и** (сім**ох**)	трина дцят**и/ьох**	п'ят десят**и/ьох**
Dative	сем**и** (сім**ом**)	трина дцят **и/ьом**	п'ят десят **и/ьом**
Accusative	сім (сім**ох**)	трина дцять **/ох**	п'ят десят **/ьох**
Instrumental	сь**ома** (сім**ома**)	трина дцять **ма/ома**	п'ят десять **ма/ома**
Locative	сем**и** (сім**ох**)	трина дцят **и/ьох**	п'ят десят **и/ьох**

Stresses are underlined

4. Declining of numerals сорок (40), дев'яносто (90), сто (100)

Case	40	90	100
Nominative	сорок	дев'яносто	сто
Genitive			
Dative			
Accusative			
Instrumental	сорока	дев'яноста	ста
Locative			

Stresses are underlined

5. Declining of numerals двісті-чотириста (200-400) and with -сот

Declining these numerals will change both their parts. Though written together these numerals are pronounced as separate words.

Case	200	300	500
Nominative	двісті	триста	п'ятсот
Genitive	двохсот	трьохсот	п'ятисот
Dative	двомстам	трьомстам	п'ятистам
Accusative	двісті	триста	п'ятсот
Instrumental	двомастами	трьомастами	п'ятьмастами (п'ятьомастами)
Locative	двохстах	трьохстах	п'ятистах

Stresses are underlined

6. Declining of numerals тисяча (1,000), мільйон (1,000,000), мільярд (1,000,000,000), нуль (0)

Case	0		1000	
	Singular	Plural	Singular	Plural
Nominative	нуль	нул_і	т_исяча	т_исячі
Genitive	нул_я	нул_ів	т_исячі	т_исяч
Dative	нул_ю/_еві	нул_ям	т_исячі	т_исячам
Accusative	нуль	нул_і	т_исячу	т_исячі
Instrumental	нул_ем	нул_ями	т_исячею	т_исячами
Locative	нул_ю/_еві	нул_ях	т_исячі	т_исячах

Case	1000000		1000000000	
	Singular	Plural	Singular	Plural
Nominative	мільй_он	мільй_они	мільй_ярд	мільй_ярди
Genitive	мільй_она	мільй_онів	мільй_ярда	мільй_ярдів
Dative	мільй_ону/_ові	мільй_онам	мільй_ярду/_ові	мільй_ярдам
Accusative	мільй_он	мільй_они	мільй_ярд	мільй_ярди
Instrumental	мільй_оном	мільй_онами	мільй_ярдом	мільй_ярдами
Locative	мільй_оні/_ові	мільй_онах	мільй_ярді/_ові	мільй_ярдах

Stresses are underlined

7. Declining of assembled numerals

When declining these numerals have the same forms as the corresponding cardinal numerals, but only secondary ones (which are in brackets).

Case	7
Nominative	се́меро
Genitive	сімо́х
Dative	сімо́м
Accusative	сімо́х
Instrumental	сімома́
Locative	сімо́х

Stresses are underlined

8. Declining of fractions

When declining fractions, the first part changes as cardinal and second as ordinal numeral.

Case	1/2
Nominative	одна́ дру́га
Genitive	одніє́ї (одно́ї) дру́гої
Dative	одні́й дру́гій
Accusative	одну́ дру́гу
Instrumental	одніє́ю (одно́ю) дру́гою
Locative	одні́й дру́гій

Stresses are underlined

9. Declining of ordinal numbers

Ordinal numeral *третій (третя, третє, треті)* decline like adjectives from <u>soft group</u> and the rest decline like adjectives from <u>hard group</u>.

10. Declining of composite cardinal numerals

When declining composite cardinals every numeral changes.

Case	345
Nominative	триста сорок п'ять
Genitive	трьохсот сорока п'яти
Dative	трьомстам сорокам п'ятьом
Accusative	триста сорок п'ять
Instrumental	трьомастами сорока п'ятьма
Locative	трьохстах сорока п'яти

Stresses are underlined

11. Declining of composite ordinal numerals

When declining composite ordinals only last numeral changes.

Case	139th
Nominative	сто тридцять дев'ятий
Genitive	сто тридцять дев'ятого
Dative	сто тридцять дев'ятому
Accusative	сто тридцять дев'ятий/ого
Instrumental	сто тридцять дев'ятим
Locative	сто тридцять дев'ятому

Stresses are underlined

Numerals: rules for numerals and nouns

Here are some rules on how to use numerals and nouns in pairs:

- After numeral *one* (even if it is a part of a composite numeral) noun has **Nominative singular** form:

  21 день, двадцять один день (21 days);

  41 дерево, сорок одне дерево (41 trees);

  1 151 зірка, тисяча сто п'ятдесят одна зірка (1 151 stars).

- After numerals *two and more* noun has plural form:

  дві ручки (two pens),

  вісім комп'ютерів (eight computers),

  шістдесят років (sixty years).

- After numerals *two*, *three*, *four* (even if they are a part of a composite numeral) noun has **Nominative plural** form:

  32 метри, тридцять два метри (thirty-two metres);

53 олівці, п'ятдесят три олівці (fifty-three pencils);

364 дні, триста шістдесят чотири дні (three hundred sixty-four days)

Exceptions:

Nouns that loose their *-ин-* suffix in plural form and fourth declension nouns after numerals *two*, *three*, *four* have **Genitive singular** form:

селя<u>нин</u> — a villager, sing. — селяни — pl.;

селянина — sing., Genitive case.

42 селянина, сорок два селянина (forty-two villagers).

ім'я — a name, sing., Nominative case,

імені — sing., Genitive case.

2 імені, два імені (two names);

кошеня — a kitten, sing., Nominative case,

кошеняти — sing., Genitive case.

4 кошеняти, чотири кошеняти (four kittens).

- After numerals *five* **and more** nouns have **Genitive plural** form:

5 сантиметрів, п'ять сантиметрів (five centimetres);

14 кроків, чотирнадцять кроків (fourteen steps);

26 питань, двадцять шість питань (twenty-six questions);

365 днів, триста шістдесят днів (three hundred sixty-five days);

87 кілометрів, вісімдесят сім кілометрів (eighty seven kilometres).

- After assembled numerals (except *обидва*) nouns have **Genitive plural** form:

двоє кошенят (two kittens),

троє чоловіків (three men),

шестеро дверей (six doors).

After *обидва, обидві* — **Nominative plural**:

обидва брати (both brothers),

обидві жінки (both women).

- After numerals *two*, *three*, *four* adjectives usually have **Nominative plural** form (like the noun): чотири дерев'яні столи (four wooden tables),

  дві золоті монети (two golden coins).

  However, near the <u>neuter nouns</u> adjectives often have **Genitive plural** form:

  два зелених дерева (two green trees),

  три чистих вікна (three clean windows).

- After numerals *тисяча, мільйон, мільярд, нуль* nouns always have **Genitive plural** form:

  a thousand thoughts: тисяча думок (Nom., sing.; Gen., pl.), тисячею думок (Inst., sing.; Gen., pl.);

  a million people: мільйон людей (Nom., sing.; Gen., pl.), мільйонами людей (Inst., pl.; Gen., pl.).

- After *fractions* nouns always have **Genitive singular** form:

  півтори години (one and a half hour),

  півтора року (one and a half year).

- *Names of the months* always have **Genitive** form:

  May 3: третє травня (Nom.; Gen.), третього травня (Gen.; Gen.), з третім травня (Inst.; Gen.).

The Pronoun

The pronoun (займенник /zɑjmɛ'n:ɪk/) is a part of speech which defines objects, qualities or quantities, without naming them.

They answer the questions: *who? what? which? whose? how many?*

Pronouns have genders, singular/plural form and change according to cases.

There are nine groups of pronouns in Ukrainian language:

1. Personal pronouns (особові займенники): **я** (I), **ти** (you), **він, вона, воно** (he/she/it), **ми** (we), **ви** you), **вони** (they);

2. Possessive pronouns (присвійні займенники) **мій** (my/mine), **твій** (you/yours), **його, її** (his/its, her/hers), **наш** (our/ours), **ваш** (your/yours), **їхній** (their/theirs), **свій**;

3. Reflexive pronouns (зворотні займенники): **себе** (myself/herself/himself/herself/itself/ourselves/themselves/yourselves/oneself);

4. Interrogative pronouns (питальні займенники): **хто?** (who?), **що?** (what?), **чий?** (whose?), **який?** (what?), **котрий?** (which? what?);

5. Conjunctive pronouns (відносні займенники): **хто** (who), **що** (what), **чий** (whose), **який** (what), **котрий** (which, what);

6. Demonstrative pronouns (вказівні займенники): **цей** (this), **той** (that), **такий** (such), **стільки** (this much);

7. Defining pronouns (означальні займенники): **всякий, усякий** (every; any), **весь, увесь, ввесь** (all; whole), **кожний, кожен** (every), **інший** (another), **сам** (self; alone), **самий** (the one; the same);

8. Indefinite pronouns (неозначені займенники): **хтось** (somebody), **щось** (something), **хто-небудь** (somebody), **будь-який** (anything), **будь-хто** (anybody), **будь-що** (anything) etc.;

9. Negative pronouns (заперечні займенники): **ніхто** (nobody; no one), **ніщо** (nothing), **ніякий** (no; none; any), **нічий** (nobody's), **ніскільки** (not at all; not a bit; nothing).

1/ **Personal pronouns** define people, other creatures, objects, things.

All personal pronouns change according to cases and have singular, plural forms. Pronoun *він* also has genders

я — I (sing.)

ти — you (sing.)

він — he (sing., masculine)

вона — she (sing., feminine)

воно — it (sing., neuter)

ми — we (pl.)

вони — they (pl.)

ви — you (pl.)

2/ **Possessive pronouns** define possession of an object to the first person: **мій** (my/mine), to the second: **твій** (your/yours), **ваш** (your/yours), the third: **його** (his, its), **її** (her/hers), **наш** (our/ours), **їхній** (their/theirs) or any person: **свій**.

Possessive pronouns *(except його, її)* change according to cases, genders and have singular, plural forms.

But unlike other possessive pronouns, **свій** is used to describe the belonging of an object to any person, which is performing an action.

For example:

Він продає свої книги. — He is selling his books (he as a person is performing an action - selling);

Його книжки дуже відомі. — His books are very popular (there isn't any action here).

3/ **Reflexive pronoun себе** defines someone, who is performing an action. It does not have gender, singular/plural or Nominative forms, but has other case forms. Reflexive pronoun can be used for any person, one or many. This is basically all English reflexive pronouns in one. *Myself, herself, himself, herself, itself, ourselves, themselves, yourselves, oneself* will all mean *себе* in Ukrainian.

Він себе не розуміє. — He does not understand himself.

Дівчата себе не впізнали. — Girls did not recognise themselves.

Вона купила собі нове дзеркало. — She bought herself a new mirror.

4/ **Interrogative pronouns** consist of a question about a person (**хто?** who?), an object (**що?** what?), quality (**чий?** whose? **який?** what? **котрий?** which? what?), quantity (**скільки?** how many?).

хто, що, скільки change according to cases;

чий, який, котрий change according to cases, genders and have singular/plural forms.

Хто ця жінка? — Who is this woman?

Кого ти шукаєш? — Whom are you looking for? (*кого?* is a Accusative form of *хто?*)

Що ви робите? — What are you doing?

Чия це сумка? — Whose bag is this?

Які книжки ви читаєте? — What books do you read?

Котра зараз година? — What (Which) time is it now?

Скільки тут правил? — How many rules are there?

The difference between *що? (what?)* and *який? (what?)*, *котрий? (which? what?)* lies within their purpose.

що? (what?) serves to ask about an object in opposite to *хто? who?*:

Хто це? (Who is this?) — Що це? (What is this?)

Кого ти тут знаєш (Who do you know here?) — Що ти тут маєш? (What do you have here?)

який? (what?) serves to ask about the quality of a person or an object (mostly):

Які книжки вам подобаються? (What books do you like?)

Який ваш улюблений предмет? (What is your favourite subject?)

котрий? (which? what?) serves to ask about quality as well, but the answer is mostly an ordinal numeral which points out the order of the object in the queue.

Котра година? (What time is it (now)?) — Восьма. (Eight o'clock.)

Котрі у нас місця? (What seats do we have?) — Дев'яте та десяте. (Ninth and tenth.)

5/ **Conjunctive pronouns** the same as interrogative pronouns but without question-marks. They are used according to the same rules as the corresponding interrogative pronouns.

Я знаю, <u>хто</u> ти. — I know <u>who</u> you are.

Олівець, <u>який</u> ти мені дав, дуже гострий. — The pencil <u>that</u> you gave me is very sharp.

They serve as connections between independent and relative clauses.

6/ **Demonstrative pronouns** define: an object/person — **цей** (this), **той** (that); quality — **такий** (such); quantity — **стільки** (this much).

Pronouns *цей, той, такий* change according to genders, cases and have singular/plural forms (like adjectives). Pronoun *стільки* change according to cases only.

7/ **Defining pronouns** define the quality in general: **весь, увесь, ввесь** (all; whole; everybody); **всякий, усякий** (every; any); **кожний, кожен** (every); **інший** (another); **сам** (self; alone); **самий** (the one; the same). They change according to genders, cases and have singular/plural forms (like adjectives).

весь, увесь, ввесь defines the completeness of an object or gathering of objects while *всякий, усякий, кожний, кожен* in return define separate objects in a certain gathering:

Завтра <u>всі</u> поїдуть додому. — Tomorrow <u>everybody (all)</u> will go home.

<u>Кожен</u> учень повинен знати розклад. — <u>Every</u> student has to know schedule.

інший defines the difference between objects that are being a part of one gathering:

Йому потрібен <u>інший</u> репетитор з математики. — He needs <u>another</u> Math tutor.

Pronoun *сам* emphasizes on the independent role of a specific object. This pronoun is a part of many words (around five hundred) what gives them a reversive or independent meaning: самоаналіз (self-analysis), самозахист (self-defence), самознищення (self-destruction), самовираження (self-expression) etc.

In idioms сам is often combined with a reflexive pronoun себе:

бути самим собою — to be yourself,

сам собі господар — (to be) your own master,

сам собі ворог — (to be) your own enemy,

сам собі ворог — (to be) your own enemy,

8/ **Indefinite pronouns** define the unknown (indefinite) person, object, quality, quantity: *хтось* (somebody), *щось* (something), *хто-небудь* (somebody; anybody), *будь-який* (anything), *будь-хто* (anybody), *будь-що* (anything) etc. They are made by adding particles **будь-, -небудь, аби-, де-, -сь, казна-, хтозна-** to the interrogative pronouns with a hyphen (except -*сь*).

хто + небудь = хто-небудь,

що + сь = щось,

казна + що = казна-що (who knows what).

Тут хтось є? — Is anyone (someone) here?

Мені потрібно щось купити. — I need to buy something.

Він повірить у <u>будь-що</u>. — He will believe in <u>anything</u>.

9/ **Negative pronouns** define the absence of a person, an object, qualities, quantity: **ніхто** (nobody; no one), **ніщо** (nothing), **ніякий** (no; none; any), **нічий** (nobody's), **ніскільки** (not at all; not a bit; nothing). They are made by adding particle **ні-** to the interrogative pronouns and are written together.

ні + хто? = ніхто,

ні + що? = ніщо,

ні + який? = ніякий,

ні + чий? = нічий,

ні + скільки? = ніскільки.

Він <u>нічого</u> не пам'ятає. — He doesn't remember anything. (He remembers <u>nothing</u>.)

If there is a preposition between particle and pronoun then they all are written separately.

Це не було несподіванкою <u>ні для кого</u>. — This wasn't a surprise for anyone. (This was a surprise <u>for no one</u>.)

The Pronoun: Cases

	I	we	you (singular)	you (plural)
Nominative	я	ми	ти	ви
Genitive	мене	нас	тебе	вас
Dative	мені	нам	тобі	вам
Accusative	мене	нас	тебе	вас
Instrumental	мною	нами	тобою	вами
Locative	мені	нас	тобі	вас

	he	it	she	they
Nominative	він	воно	вона	вони
Genitive[1]	його		її	їх
	prep. + нього		*prep.* + неї	*prep.* + них
Dative	йому		їй	їм
Accusative[1]	його		її	їх
	prep. + нього		*prep.* + неї	*prep.* + них
Instrumental	ним		неї	ними
Locative [1,2]	*prep.* + ньому		*prep.* +	*prep.* +
	prep. + нім		ній	них

я [jɑ] — I (sing.); ти [tɪ] — you (sing.); він [wʲin] — he (sing., masculine); вона [wɔn'ɑ] — she (sing., feminine); воно [wɔn'ɔ] — it (sing., neuter); ми [mɪ] — we (pl.); вони [wɔn'ɪ] — they (pl.); ви [wɪ] — you (pl.).

Okay. I think that's more than enough grammar! It's actually far more than you will need to speak Ukrainian but I have included as much as possible because it will help you with your reading and writing which in turn help will help with *speaking* Ukrainian.

It is best not to try to learn this all at once but to take what you need. Use the grammar section for reference only.

Strangely, learning Ukrainian grammar will also help you with English grammar.

You don't need to know everything, though. If you're unsure about the difference between a subordinating conjunction and a coordinating conjunction, you'll probably be OK unless you're a teacher or a grammar textbook author.

But at a minimum, it's best to brush up on these ideas:

- noun
- pronoun
- adjective
- verb
- preposition
- participle
- definite and indefinite articles

You should also familiarize yourself with the idea of an **auxiliary verb**, **conjugation** and the concept of **tenses**.

1. Monitor your progress and be consistent

This actually applies to many aspects of language learning, but it can be especially important for learning the nuts and bolts of a language.

If you want to learn something new, you'll have to dedicate time to it. The more time, the better, and the more consistent you are with that time, the better. But if you can only do 20 minutes a day, four days a week, that's still probably more effective than 90 minutes in one breakneck Ukrainian-cramming session. Your brain needs time to absorb what you've learned.

At the same time, record new vocabulary, new questions and new thoughts in some way. If you like to listen to music or watch classic movies, (go to FluentU where they have classic Ukrainian movies which are ideal for learning Ukrainian) you may still learn well, but most people find that by writing down new vocabulary words, for example, they retain a lot more of the new vocabulary that they've been learning. It also lets them monitor how far they've come and identify areas for future learning.

CHAPTER EIGHT

MOTIVATION *(yawn)*

I don't know about you, but I usually need some pretty strong motivation just to get out of bed in the morning. Maybe, its age... But I'm wandering off topic (onset of senility, no doubt). With me, it's usually the slow dawning of hunger and the yearning for caffeine, usually in tea form. If I can be bothered, I make it with (proper) loose tea in a teapot and pour it in to a bone china cup with a saucer. Why do I sometimes make it with a teabag in a mug and sometimes in a teapot and served in a china cup and saucer (a Royal Albert tea service if you must know).? Well, for one thing, it tastes a lot better when I make it with "proper" brewed tea and serve it in chinaware, but that really isn't the answer, as just dropping a teabag in a mug still produces a good cup of tea and saves a hell of a lot of time and messing about. The answer is really that when I can be bothered to make *real* tea it is usually tied in with that thing called "motivation".

I do have specific reasons for choosing to make real tea most mornings, which I will not bore you with. Some are practical and others are sentimental. The mornings when I don't make real tea also have their own fewer specific reasons, usually involving lack of time, or simply that I can't be bothered.

Sit back for a moment with pen and paper and list the reasons you would like to be able to speak Ukrainian. Some reasons will spring readily to mind and will go at the top of your list, but others you might have to search a little deeper for and these are equally important. Have the list at hand, on a bedside table, perhaps, and give it a glance before going to sleep and upon awakening. The list may change after a while, but the reasons will be equally as important. They are your motivation, and you should reinforce them every day.

You don't have to use the same list all the time and writing it is just as important as reading it. Here is one that helps you to be positive about what you are doing. It is quite long as I have illustrated each point with an explanation, which you won't have to do as you will know what you mean. Feel free to take what you want from the list for your own use but don't forget to add your own. Only you know what really motivates you. I am indebted to Henrik Edberg from The Positivity Blog for the following list.

Get started and let the motivation catch up.
If you want to work in a consistent way every day, then sometimes you have to get going despite not feeling motivated. The funny thing I've discovered is that after I've worked for a while, things feel easier and easier, and the motivation catches up with me.

Start small if big leads to procrastination.
If a project or task feels too big and daunting, don't let that lead you into procrastination. Instead, break it down into

small steps and then take just one of them to start moving forward.

Start tiny if a small step doesn't work.
If breaking it down and taking a small step still leads you to procrastinate, then go even smaller. Take just a tiny one-to-two minute step forward.

Reduce the daily distractions.
Shut the door to your office or where you are learning. Put your smart-phone on silent mode. If you are a serial web surfer use an extension for your browser like StayFocusd to keep yourself on track.

Get accountability from people in your life.
Tell your friends and family what you are doing. Ask one or more to regularly check up on you and your progress. By doing this, you'll be a lot less likely to weasel out of things or give up at the first obstacle.

Get motivation from people in your life.
Spend less time with negative people. Instead, spend more of the time you have now freed up with enthusiastic or motivated people and let their energy flow over to you.

Get motivation from people you don't know.
Don't limit yourself to just motivation you can get from the people closest to you. There is a ton of motivating books, podcasts, blogs, and success stories out there that you can tap into to up or renew your motivation.

Play music that gives you energy.

One of the simplest things to do when you are low in energy or motivation is to play music that is upbeat and/or inspires in some way. In the case of learning Ukrainian, play some Ukrainian music that have lyrics. There are also a lot of Ukrainian-speaking radio stations online. I will come to those later, but for the moment, you can just run a search on Google and choose one that suits your tastes.

Find the optimism.

A positive and constructive way of looking at things can energize and recharge your motivation. So, when you're in what looks like a negative situation, ask yourself questions like, "What's one thing that's good about this?" and, "What's one hidden opportunity here?"

Be kind to yourself when you stumble.

Don't fall into the trap of beating yourself when you stumble or fail. You'll just feel worse and less motivated. Instead, try this the next time: be kind to yourself, nudge yourself back on the path you were on, and take one small step forward.

Be constructive about the failures.

When you stumble ask yourself, "What's one thing I can learn from this setback?" Then keep that lesson in mind and take action on it to improve what you do.

Compare yourself to yourself.

See how far you've come instead of deflating yourself and your motivation by comparing yourself to others who are so far ahead of you.

Compete in a friendly way.

If you have a friend also learning Ukrainian make it a friendly competition to learn some task first. The element of competition tends to liven things up. You could also add a small prize for extra motivation and to spice things up.

Remind yourself why.

When you're feeling unmotivated it's easy to lose sight of why you're doing something, so take two minutes and write down your top three reasons for wanting to learn Ukrainian. Put that note where you'll see it every day.

Remember what you're moving away from.

Motivate yourself to get going by looking at the negative impact of not learning another language. Imagine where you will be in a year if you continue to learn. Imagine where you will be in five years if you continue to learn. Don't throw it away by giving up.

Be grateful for what you've got.

To put your focus on what you still have and who you are, ask yourself a question like, "What are three things I sometimes take for granted but can be grateful for in my life?" One possible answer could be: "I have a roof over my head, clean water to drink, and food to eat.

Mix things up.

A rut will kill motivation, so mix things up. Make a competition out of a task with yourself

Declutter your workspace.

Take a couple of minutes to clean your workspace up. I find that having an uncluttered and minimalistic workspace helps me to think more clearly, and I feel more focused and ready to tackle the next task.

Reduce your to-do list to just one item.
An over-stuffed to-do list can be a real motivation killer, so reduce it to the one that's most important to you right now (hopefully, learning Ukrainian), or the one you've been procrastinating doing. If you like, have another list with tasks to do later on and tuck it away somewhere where you can't see it.

Don't forget about the breaks.
If you are working from home try working for 45 minutes each hour and use the rest for a break where you eat a snack or get out for some fresh air. You'll get more done in a day and week and do work of higher quality because your energy, focus, and motivation will simply last longer.

Adjust your goal size.
If a big goal in your life feels overwhelming, set a smaller goal. And if a smaller goal doesn't seem inspiring, try to aim higher and make it a bigger goal and see how that affects your motivation.

Exercise.
Working out doesn't just affect your body. It releases inner tensions and stress and makes you more focused once again.

Take two minutes to look back at successes.

Close your eyes and let the memories of your biggest successes - no matter in what part of your life - wash over you. Let those most positive memories boost your motivation.

Celebrate successes (no matter the size).
If you're looking forward to a nice reward that you're giving yourself after you're done with a task, then your motivation tends to go up. So, dangle those carrots to keep your motivation up.

Do a bit of research before you get started.
Learning from people who have gone where you want to go and done what you want to do can help you to avoid pitfalls and give you a realistic time-table for success.

Take a two minute meditation break.
In the afternoons - or when needed - sit down with closed eyes and just focus 100% on your breathing for two minutes. This clears the mind and releases inner tensions.

Go out in nature.
Few things give as much energy and motivation to take on life as this does. Go out for a walk in the woods or by the sea. Just spend a moment with nature and, the fresh air and don't think about anything special.
What about learning a bit of Ukrainian while just laying on the sofa?

Coffee Break Ukrainian
This laid-back podcast: coffebreak languages (https://coffeebreaklanguages.com/) does exactly what it says

on the tin. The lively presenters give you very small snippets designed to feel "like going for a coffee with your friend who happens to speak Ukrainian". The podcasts go through the basics at beginner level right through to advanced conversations and are perfect for listening to while snuggled up on the sofa with a cup of something delicious. The basic podcast version is free for all levels.

(https://coffeebreaklanguages.com/category/one-minute-ukrainian/)

CHAPTER NINE

BEST UKRAINIAN TV SHOWS

Have you ever thought about learning Ukrainian by watching Ukrainian-speaking TV shows?

Instead of sitting in a classroom memorizing irregular verbs, you could be learning Ukrainian by sitting on the couch in your pajamas, munching popcorn.

But if it were really that easy, wouldn't everyone be speaking Ukrainian by now?

And come to think of it, wouldn't you have already done it?

Watching Ukrainian TV shows is a way of *adding* to your learning, but there are some pitfalls to watch out for. And you need strategies to make sure that you learn as much Ukrainian as possible while you watch.

In this chapter, we will look at the best Ukrainian TV shows on Netflix, Amazon Prime and Apple (if you do not have access to these platforms, you can use YouTube). There is one important thing to bear in mind though, they are rare, so look out for them and prize them when you find them—they are treasures that will prove a great aid to your learning.

Note: At the time of writing the Russian invasion of the Ukraine is taking place so there will be plenty of newscasts in Ukrainian. However, this sad event will give you plenty of opportunities to improve your Ukrainian and give you an added insight into the invasion itself. This is not a political book, it is a language-learning book, so I will make no further comments on the conflict.

Learn how to make the most out of these Ukrainian TV shows. This includes:

- How to choose the right series so you'll get addicted to Ukrainian TV—and to learning Ukrainian!
- What to do when you don't understand (a common problem that's easy to solve when you know how).
- More than just chilling out: study activities to boost your learning with Ukrainian TV shows.

By watching Ukrainian TV shows, you'll constantly be improving your listening skills. And if you use the subtitles in Ukrainian, you'll also improve your reading and pick up vocabulary more easily. It'll even improve your speaking as you'll get used to hearing common phrases over and over, and they'll come to you more easily when you need them in conversation

Best of all, you'll be learning and enjoying yourself at the same time!

At this point, you might be thinking, "Sounds great, but I've already tried listening to Ukrainian TV shows, and I didn't understand anything."

And even if you do understand bits and pieces, watching TV in a foreign language can feel overwhelming. Where should you start? How do you know if you're learning?
By the end of this chapter, you'll have all the answers.

Learning a new language can become repetitive and bothersome after a while. So thank goodness for TV shows that help us learn languages in a creative, entertaining and fun way.

Watching Ukrainian TV shows will allow you to hear the different dialects, increase your vocabulary and get used to the pronunciation. It will also allow you to learn more about Ukrainian culture.

Below are the best TV shows in order to learn Ukrainian:

Servant of the People (Sluga narodu)

Comedy (2015-2019)

After a Ukrainian high school teacher's tirade against government corruption goes viral on social media, he finds himself elected the country's new president.

The Silence

Crime, Drama, Mystery (2021 -)
Dramatic events unfold in Croatia and Ukraine. The first girl drowned, the second one died from a drug overdose. The main suspect in these deaths, however, soon turns out to be innocent - and dead too. While detective Vladimir and reporter Stribor struggle to solve these murders in Croatia, the niece of Olga, an Ukrainian philanthropist, goes missing in Kyiv. Olga's Croatian husband, Ivan Hrvatic, one of the most influential people in the city of Osijek, undertakes to help the investigation. But the missing girl is found dead - in Osijek, not in Kyiv. And she is now the third victim. It looks as if a serial killer is operating in Croatia. Vladimir, Stribor and Olga will eventually get to the truth, but not before each of them pays a high price for it. Reporter Stribor will have to trade off his moral principles, and detective Vladimir may have to put his ex-wife in prison for murder. And Olga's happy marriage will soon be under threat because of the shocking story of trafficking weapons and young girls to Europe.

The Sniffer

Action, Crime, Drama (2013 -)

They call him the Sniffer. He's the proud owner of an acute sense of smell, he knows things about you even you don't and would rather keep to yourself.

Mata Hari

Drama, History (2016 - 2017)

A sex icon becomes a spy during one of the most important wars of the 20th century.

Love in Chains

Drama, Romance (2019 -)

Katerina Verbitskaya was raised as a noble lady with her godmother Anna Chervinskaya but for the whole world she was only the property of Peter Chervinsky. She falls in love with the nobleman Alexey Kosach who knows nothing about her origin. On the way to freedom and love, the serf maid will have to overcome a lot of trials.

64 Zoo Lane

Animation, Family (1919 - 2013)

64 Zoo Lane is a kid show about a girl who goes outside her house at night to play with her zoo friends including a giraffe, zebra and more. The show is definitely a show for the whole family to watch.

School

Drama, (2018 - 2019)

Successful businesswoman Katya finds out that her daughter tried to commit suicide. As it turned out, not the first time. To be closer to her daughter and understand what the kids really wants she becomes a teacher.

The Slavs

Adventure, Fantasy (2021 -)

A young girl called Draha is different than her peers because she's conscious and ambitious. During her self-discovery, she is accompanied by a mysterious stranger that she saved and is slowly becoming a member of the fort Big table.

Saga

Drama, (2020)

The story of the Kozaks starts before the First World War. Throughout the century, the Kozaks, together with the whole nation, live through various hardships and challenges Ukraine undergoes. They go through the wars, Holodomor and changes of political agendas - The only thing that helps them survive in this whirl is a strong foundation that's held the family all these years: "Whatever happens, we're the family." Frequently this basis of the "family code" undergoes challenges. Rivalry in love, differences in worldviews, little and huge combats - the Kozaks have to go through all of them, and so do millions of other Ukrainian families - What's waiting for the Kozaks in the future? Can they preserve their unique world in which there's enough place for everything - laughter, tears, self-sacrifice, betrayal and big love that has been protecting and uniting the family for generations?

Vangeliya

Biography, Drama (2013 -)

1996 Russia. A government subsidized delegation heads to Bulgaria to meet the prophet and contemporary marvel-Vanga. A TV crew joins the delegates hoping to interview the extraordinary woman. Among the group, Vanga singles out an intern, Alisa, who will bear witness to Vanga's heart-rending confession. As the woman's narrative slowly unfolds, we discover a love lost in the midst of war, numerous hardships during the post-war period and learn the secret of Vanga's mysterious past. The events will intertwine with key figures in the history of mankind: Adolph Hitler, Josef Stalin, Yuri Gagarin. Vanga weaves the story into an elaborate net of interconnected events which spiral into a fixed past, the immediate present but a future open to those willing to see.

Nichto ne sluchaetsya dvazhdy

Drama, Romance (2019 -)

This story begins 20 years ago. A small military settlement on the very border seems quiet and peaceful only at first glance. A small country with its own rules, where there is a place for passion, love, loyalty and betrayal.

The Red Queen

Drama, (2015 -)

Story of the rise of a girl from proverbial humble beginnings to top Russian fashion model during Cold War-era USSR.

Hide and Seek

Crime, Drama, Thriller (2019 -)

In an ordinary looking apartment, a father and daughter play a game of hide-and-seek. While searching for his daughter, she is nowhere to be found - Later, a video is posted which shows the girl holding a sign with a mysterious set of numbers. But what do they mean? She's the first of several children who disappear without a trace in a small industrial town. Young detectives Varta Naumova and Maksim Shumov take on the complex case and - their own demons. Varta is a distant person and extremely protective of her personal space, while Maksim comes across as an easy-going sociable guy. Both have experienced trauma in their lives, and this case touches them on a deeper level. They become personally vested in finding the children and apprehending the kidnapper as they face their respective pasts.

The Voice of Ukraine

Music, Reality-TV (2011 -)

Golos Krainy (The Voice of Ukraine) on Channel 1+1 is the main vocal show of Ukraine, which searches for singing talents. The talents will be mentored by the star coaches and the viewers will decide who will be the best voice of the country.

Na tvoey storone

Drama, (2019 -)

The series is based on the classic story of Beauty and the Beast. It is a story of constructive love. The protagonist, a well-known 30-year-old cardiac surgeon Nastya, tries to help her beloved Maksym, who for many years has been part of criminal circles, out of the hell he lives in. The woman does not suspect that the owner of the clinic where she works is indeed a criminal. Apart from running the hospital and helping people, he has an unlawful business that deals in illegal medicines and drugs. Once, Nastya by accident witnesses a murder his gang commits. It is now clear she is doomed: the boss orders his thugs to kill her. However, the boss' nephew, who is also his chief bodyguard, disobeys the order. To save Nastya's life he proposes her to marry him. Thus a decent woman becomes a member of a big criminal family and starts living with all of them in their huge mansion, which hides a lot of secrets. But the hardest role Nastya has to play is to be Maksym's wife. They are complete antipodes: Nastya is a saint, while Maksym is a sinner, she is good, while he is evil, she is the light, while he is the darkness. Nevertheless, Nastya can see Maksym's true self through the shell of indifference and cruelty that covers him. She can awoke his heart, clear his soul and change his life.

The Voice Kids (Ukraine)

Game-Show, Music (2012 -)

There are three coaches, who are all famous in the music industry. During the blind auditions (Vybir Naoslip) these coaches will turn around in their chairs when they hear a performer up to the age 14, they want in their team. If there are more coaches who want the same performer, he or she gets to choose who they want as their coach. During the battles (Boi) there will be two or three contestants from the same team up against each other. The coach then has to choose one of them to get through to the live finale.

Brave Bunnies

Animation, Family (2021 -)

Brave Bunnies is an animated entertaining and educational 2D series for preschool kids (52 episodes, 7 minutes each). The main idea of the series is to show kids the diversity of the world around them, teach them to accept various traits of others and successfully communicate even with those who are completely different. Using the example of Brave Bunnies and their friends, parents can explain how to interact with other kids in the kindergarten or at the playground. In each episode, Brave Bunnies meet friends and come up with a fun game to play together.

Papik

Comedy, Drama, Romance (2019 -)

A forgotten elderly actor's only 'capital' is debts for the apartment and savings for his funeral. Tired of his dull life, he wants to part with it beautifully, so he goes to a barbershop and gets a stylish haircut and hipster beard. He then goes to a nightclub and meets a spectacular girl—a gold-digger who takes him for a millionaire.

Kozaky. Absolyutno brekhlyva istoriya

Adventure, (2020 -)

Raised by a Polish aristocrat, Ivan is a young Ukrainian man of humble peasant origins. His cheeky nature pushes him to rob the Moscow Tsar of precious jewels, yet it's to a noble end: he needs the royal riches to free his mother from Ottoman enslavement. But then it turns out that the simple robbery is not that simple: Ivan accidentally steals a magical heirloom, an earring which had helped the Moscow ruler to stave off defeat. The magic earring ends up in Ukrainian Cossack Fortress, aka the Sich, what's worse - it's in the ear of the Sich leader, Koshovy. Stealing the earring from the Tsar was tricky; stealing it from the Cossacks is impossible, however hard Ivan tries to to get into their good graces. It does not help that Koshovy's right-hand man, Nazar, doesn't trust Ivan. He is also suspicious (and for a good reason) of Ivan's intentions towards Nazar's beloved Mariana. Can this get worse? It can - when the Tsar's most merciless henchman, Fedor, decides to chase and punish the thief of the heirloom personally. And the earring? - You will discover it holds more than one secret.

1941

War, (2009 -)

June, 1941. A small Russian village at the border is living its everyday life - people work, love, squabble, make plans for the future. The war changes all plans, tears families apart, the first victims fall... Some Russian straggling soldiers who managed to stay alive after the first onslaught of the German army make their own war, some of the locals joining them to avenge their murdered relatives and to fight for their native land. The villagers are rent between the threats and executions introduced by the German invaders for helping the guerrillas and the necessity to help these guerrillas who are of their own flesh and blood. German repressions meet stubborn resistance. Walter, a German lieutenant, feels that the tactics of repression are wrong, but his superiors do not understand him. Walter falls in love with a local peasant girl, Dasha, but for Dasha only one man exists - Grigory, head of the local guerrillas. Grigory in his turn is married to Alyona, but not of his won accord. Alyona knows nothing about Grigory's fate after the war begins, and helps a wounded Russian soldier hiding him from the Germans... How will the war cut all these knots?

Bessmertnik

Drama, Romance, (2015 -)

Nadya and her stepsister Irina love Igor. When Igor's sister dies after getting hit by Irina's car, Irina and her father frame Nadya and get her sentenced for three years of imprisonment.

Who Are You?

Crime (2018)

A story of psychologist Inga Stefan, who, after mysterious deaths of a couple of her patients and the disappearance of her fiance, starts working in the field of criminal profiling. Along with her own investigation, Inga cooperates with the police homicide division. As the plot develops, Inga finds out that a maniac, who murdered her patients and fiance, has followed her for many years. Inga learns more details about the stalker what makes him happy as he craves for her attention, company, and understanding. While investigating crimes, Inga tries to put herself in the murderer's skin. She constantly asks questions about the murderer's personality, motives, and possible location. At the same time, Inga starts working with the homicide team. Together with Major Oleg Mischenko, the division chief, they go all the way from antipathy and never-ending conflicts to partnership, friendship, liking and, finally, love.

Vasiliy Stalin

Biography, Drama, History (2013)

This is the story about the son of one of the greatest tyrants of the Twentieth Century—Joseph Stalin's flesh and blood, Vasily.

Orei i reshka

Reality-TV (2011 -)

Every weekend, the two presenters go to different cities in the world. According to the rules of the program one have to live on Saturday and Sunday spending just $ 100, while the second can spend unlimited funds, which are stored on a golden card. In order to decide which of them will live like a millionaire and who will learn to survive, presenters toss a coin before each travel, and each time it is all about Heads or Tails.

To Catch the Kaidash

Comedy, Drama, (2020)

The events unfold in a remote Ukrainian village, where the Kaidash family lives, led by Omelko, who is addicted to alcohol. His wife Marusya is concerned about the future of their two adult sons, who are looking for suitable brides. In the center of the plot is the confrontation between Marusya Kaydash and young daughters-in-law, with whom she tries to get along under the same roof. The plot of the TV series is based on the social novella Kaidash's Family by Ivan Nechuy-Levytskyi.

Maski Show

Comedy, (1991-2006)

An original sitcom from Odessa. Made in the best traditions of silent comedy. Every episode tells a different story.

Drop

Drama, Romance (2021 -)

This is a story about cruelty and its consequences.

Secrets

Crime, Drama (2019)

Katya and Mykola have known each other since they were kids. Mykola's family moved to a small city called Stanov, where Katya lived with her father. While their parents tried repairing their relationship, the kids spend the most of time together. The boy and the girl first became best friends and then fell in love with each other, unconditionally and purely as all children do. However, a terrible tragedy had separated the couple.

Early Swallows

Drama, (2019 - 2020)

The series revolves around the lives of Ukrainian teenagers in a secondary school class. The teenagers struggle with bullying, including the Blue Whale Challenge, lack of parental support, suicidal behavior, LGBT identity crises-a subject that is rarely portrayed on Ukrainian television-alcoholic parents, and speech disabilities. In one of the show's main plot lines, the main characters are stalked on the Internet by an anonymous person who pretends to be their friend,

Anna German

Biography, Drama (2012 - 2013)

A dramatized biography of Anna German: a Polish singer, immensely popular in Poland and in the Soviet Union in the 1960s-1970s.

Vecherniy Kvartal

Comedy, (2005 -)

Vecherniy Kvartal is a large-scale entertainment and comedy show, performed by the acting team of Kvartal 95. Vecherniy Kvartal is an interpretation of events taking place in social and political life of the country through the prism of healthy, and sometimes - sharp political satire most recent developments in the country and in the life of each of us have become plot for funny sketches. They always laugh in Vecherniy Kvartal heartily, at politicians and athletes, musicians and TV stars, and, most often, along with them.

Gypsy Layla

Drama, (2014)

Layla the Mongrel 17-years-old gypsy Layla Rubinova desperately needs money, so she decides to rob the house of a local wealthy family, the Sviridovs. She is caught red handed by Sergey, the son of the master of the house. But instead of calling the police the young man proposes the robber - to marry him. And Layla agrees. But will the wedding happen? This is a story of a dangerous love quadrangle and after fatal events only two people, who are genuinely in love, escape it and survive, and find happiness in the end. Cutie Layla The series continues with new twists and turns of fate for the protagonist, redheaded gypsy Layla. Layla will change her name to Ekaterina, move to a different place, pick a new lifestyle and personal style. But when her dreams seem to finally come true, her past decides to remind of itself - Layla Returns Six months have passed since the events of the previous series. Layla's life has changed in many ways. After all the trials she has left the city and now lives far from civilization. Anna is the only person with whom Layla keeps in touch. Even so, she asks her not to trouble her solitude without great necessity. Six months later such necessity presents itself - the gynecologist who delivered Layla's baby is dying. On the deathbed he reveals to prison warden Gromov that he sold Layla's baby to another woman. Layla sets out to find her child.

Skazochnaya Rus

Comedy, Animation (2012 -)

Skazochnaya Rus is a unique parody comedy animated series, where events take place in fictional Fairytale Land. Modern-day well-known politicians appear as epic heroes familiar to everyone, trying to solve today's problems in a fairy tale way.

Kiss!

Drama (2013)

The calling of Natasha Bondarchuk is to make people beautiful. Since childhood she dreamt of becoming a doctor who can correct the mistakes of nature or the results of accidents. After finishing the high school she fails to enter the medical institute, so she gets the job as a medical orderly in a city hospital. There she finds the first love and the first disappointment: Dmytro Voroshilov, a handsome intern, seduces the naive girl and abandons her. Now Natasha is alone in a big city with a small child in her arms. Through perseverance, love to life and with the help of loyal friends Natasha achieves her dream. «Kiss!» is an anthem to the woman's dream, to dedication and perseverance. «Kiss. 2» is the present time story. Natasha is a mature and respectable woman. She is the director at the Beauty Institute. She raised her son Andriy to be a fine man. The challenges Natasha goes through make her stronger, she becomes tougher and colder. From a naive, charming, trustful girl she turns into a woman and a bit into a bitch. However, the shadows from the past won't let her go. She meets her first love and the father of her son, Dmytro Voroshylov who tries to resurrect the past relations. Meanwhile, by bittersweet chance, Andriy falls in love with a girl from the Voroshylov family. The circle has been closed. What can break the chain of dramatic and passionate events?

F.I.L.I.N

Crime (2020)

The investigators from a new police department work on the most complicated cases using special software called "Fillin".

Intrigues and unexpected twists make the cops face new challenges every day. In the cases they undertake more and more often are appearing the names of high-ranking police officials. The head of the department, Valentyn Smishko, can't close it down that simple, so he starts overwhelming the investigators with the cases he's sure they'll never solve and will eventually have to abandon their experiment. Thus the old system united to oppose 'Fillin'.

Ukraine's Got Talent

Reality-TV (2009 -)

Performers of all types and ages, are offered a chance to win a prize of $1 million Ukrainian Hryvnia. Top contestants are advance by 3 judges, to the finals where the audience and TV viewers will vote for a winner.

Optimus Gang

Comedy (2013 -)

A sketch comedy series about everything imaginable by ordinary guys from Kyiv.

The Realm

Action, Adventure, Drama (2021 -)

In the Carpathian mountains, a volcano has awoken, threatening the realm of Prince Daniel. In time, untold riches of the altered landscape will be revealed, and war will consume The Realm.

Perelyotnie ptitsi

Action, Drama (2014 -)

A miserable and solitary man known as Houdini lives in a small Russian town where he transports illegal immigrants over the country's border. While his criminal activities provide him with a modest income, they also bring him into contact with a large number of people from varied backgrounds, and he is hoping that one of them may be able to tell him what happened to his wife and child who went missing when the local war had broken out after the collapse of the Soviet Union. Houdini does not discriminate between the criminals, refugees, vagrants and drifters he transports into Russia until he meets a little girl one day, who pricks his conscience. Although he knows nothing about her, he decides not to give her to her 'adoptive parents' to whom he is supposed to deliver her and instead, these two lonely souls find themselves alone and on the run.

Beloved Children

Drama (2019)

After Vera retires, she decides to pay a visit to her children living in the capital city. She is sure they are successful and have achieved a lot in life. However, it turns out she is totally wrong - Her son Kostya is not a businessman at all. He has mixed up with a bad company and leads a dissipated life. Once he, drunk, runs a girl over and flees the scene. Her elder daughter Larisa, 40, used to be happy in marriage, but her husband left her for a young student. Vera's favorite child, 19-year-old Mila, has quit he university studies and now dances at a striptease club. Besides, she is pregnant from a married man. Vera stays in the city wishing to help her children solve their problems. But do adult people really want her help?

Ringer

Crime, Drama, Mystery (2019 -)

An attractive young woman, Ulyana happens to witness a murder and is forced into hiding from the killers to avoid the same fate. Her best friend who has been in love with her for many years, helps her to disappear and be rid of the dangerous pursuers. Ulyana decides to move to another city, where her rich and successful twin sister, Lera lives. The two sisters have not been in contact for a long time and, on the threshold of the reunion, Ulyana discovers that Lera has just died. When Ulyana shows up at Lera's house, Lera's husband, friends and colleagues take her for Lera. Will Ulyana be able to 'become' her twin sister and play the role perfectly?

Zatmenie

Crime, Drama, Romance (2018)

They used to study at the same school. Sveta was a straight-A beauty, while Serhii Mamaev was an obscure boy with troubles in his studies. There is nothing unusual in this story: he was extremely in love with her but she just ignored him - Twenty years later, no one dares now to call Mamayev with the casual nickname «shadow man» as they used to do at school. Sergei is an owner of a large business, he is single, many girls are around him, his daughter Anna, born out of the marriage, is 17 years old. But Svetlana lives a very simple life. She is a teacher of tango, she is happy in her marriage and has two children - Yegor of 17 and Vita of 15. Sergei randomly meets Svetlana and tries to win her heart again. Alas, she still does not care for his feelings. However this time, Sergei isn't giving up. All the time he loved Svetlana throughout all these years and has achieved success to prove that he deserves her love. She is the only woman in the world he needs - Sergei's insane desire to win Svetlana triggers a chain of tragic events in the epicenter of which is young Anya and Yegor, who met and fell in love with each other without realizing who their parents are.

Shattered Destinies

Drama, Romance (2018)

Vika is a talented designer but after her father's death, her life crumbles apart. She will only find hope in a famous fashion house immerse in chaos and turmoil. Will she be able to save her future and the company?

Ukrainian Films

Тіні забутих предків (1964)

(The Shadows of Forgotten Ancestors)

Don't mind that the title on YouTube is in Russian, since the film is completely in Ukrainian.

Have you ever thought about the alternative scenarios of Shakespeare's 'Romeo and Juliet'? 'Тіні забутих предків' is the Ukrainian answer on how Romeo could probably survive after the death of Juliet. For a long time the hero is depressed, but later, he decides he should somehow find a way to keep on living. He gets married, works hard, and tries to overcome his grief this way.

The movie is filled with Ukrainian national traditions: the burying and the wedding ceremonies, Christmas celebrations, and magic rituals. There you can get acquainted with folk songs, Carpathian nature, and the Hutsul dialect of the Ukrainian language.

Загибель богів (1988)

(The Twilight of The Gods)

What do you know about life in Soviet Ukraine? This movie shows how art, freedom, and religion were suppressed by the Soviet regime. Under suppression of religion, a brave artist intends to create an icon of the Lord's Supper. To make the icon vivid, the participants of the Supper are taken from the local people.

Soon, the artist is arrested and the local people are forced to destroy the icons.

Пропала грамота (1972)

(The Lost Document)

Can you imagine how a drunk person could win a bet with the devil? This movie is about Ukrainian Cossacks who are able to do it! Based on the texts written by Mykola Gogol, the movie shows the funny adventures of Cossacks. It starts with the cheerful folk song Танцювала риба з раком / *The Fish Was Dancing with the Crayfish,* which can be seen as a metaphor for the absurd nature of the events depicted in the film.

Такі красиві люди (2013)

(Such Beautiful People)

This modern Ukrainian movie is about people who find happiness in each day of their lives.

The heroes of the movie are beautiful because they know that love is true happiness. A couple of people who love each other more than everything else, the lonely woman-fisher and the unknown writer find their paradise at the seashore. To get acquainted with the woman-fisher, the writer jumps into the water and asks her to host him in order to dry his clothes. Then a new love story starts.

Записки кирпатого Мефістофеля (1994)

(The Notes of a Pug-nosed Mephistopheles)

What is an evil man? This movie states that, probably, the man becomes evil after losing optimistic beliefs (in the case of the main hero it is the loss of his revolutionary ideas). This story is about such types of men; it's about his women, his crimes, and his everlasting hesitation of being a father. To get rid of the former mistress, the man attempts to kill his child. However, the child survives, the current beloved woman leaves him, and his life is unpredictably changed.

Той, хто пройшов крізь вогонь (2011)

(Firecrosser)

Have you heard about Ukrainian folk magic? This movie is a great story of an aviator who was a true magician! Based on true facts, the action starts during the second World War when a young aviator demonstrates an impressing success at the specialized school. Nobody knows how he does it, but they gossip that he is a kharakternyk. Характерник is a Ukrainian magician who has supernatural skills; he's able to transform his body, to travel through time and space, to heal people, to predict the future, and even to rule wild animals.

After being imprisoned in a USSR concentration camp, the man becomes a werewolf in order to get free and save his life. Although this doomed fate takes him far away from his native land, he finds a new life at the tribe and lastly receives the news from the lost family.

To represent the Soviet atmosphere, the characters mostly talk in Russian. However, the movie has Ukrainian subtitles and is therefore helpful for Ukrainian learners to improve their language skills.

Julia Blue (2020)

Julia, a photojournalism student living in post-revolutionary Ukraine, finds her life disrupted after falling for a soldier fresh from the war zone and suffering from PTSD. As, Thelma Admas, a film critic, puts it:

"Capturing a fleeting love story in a very specific time and place one year after the 2014 revolution in Kyiv, JULIA BLUE is a different kind of war narrative. Performance driven, artistic and subtle, it is told through the eyes of a young woman who must ultimately choose the best path for her future."

Киевские фрески (1966)

(Kiev Frescoes)

Kiev Frescoes with English subtitles is a 1966 USSR short film directed by Sergei Parajanov.

Sergei Parajanov's Kiev Frescoes (Kyiv Frescos / Киевские фрески) was suppressed by Soviet Ukraine's Dovzhenko Film Studio during production in 1966, but the approximately 14 surviving minutes of Kiev Frescos nevertheless demonstrated a new film language (even more original than Shadows of Forgotten Ancestors). Paradjanov (Параджанов) later cemented this unique cinematic language in his masterpiece The Color of Pomegranates.

The Voice of the Herbs (1992)

The Voice of the Herbs an Ukrainian mystery drama film directed by Natalya Motuzko.
Based on the stories of Valery Shevchuk. The story of the initiation of a young sorceress into the secrets of magic. The film is staged in the poetic style of Ukrainian folklore.

The Lost Letter (1972)

The Lost Letter is a 1972 Ukrainian musical-tragicomedy film by Dovzhenko Film Studios in Kyiv. The movie is considered a pearl of Ukrainian cinema. The film is based on the novella The Lost Letter: A Tale Told by the Sexton of the N...Church by Nikolai Gogol from cycle Evenings on a Farm Near Dikanka.

This folk tragicomedy tells the adventures of Ukrainian cossacks Vasil and Andrij as they set out on a long journey to deliver a letter from their leader to the Russian empress in St. Petersburg.

Oxygen Starvation (1992)

Oxygen Starvation with English subtitles is a 1991 Ukrainian drama film directed by Andrij Doncik.
The Soviet army was one the worst places to be when it came to human dignity. The task of the army was to turn freethinkers into normal dumb Soviet people. An intelligent Ukrainian guy refuses to obey.

How to learn Ukrainian by watching TV shows and films

So now you've got some great Ukrainian TV shows to choose from. You can watch them as a beginner, but since they're aimed at native speakers, you'll probably enjoy them more if you're already at an intermediate level or above as you'll be able to understand more of what's being said and pick up new words without too much effort.

That said, it is possible to enjoy Ukrainian TV at lower levels, too; you just need a slightly different approach. In this section, you'll learn how to improve your Ukrainian by watching Ukrainian TV shows at any level.

You'll learn:

- How to choose the right series to get you hooked on Ukrainian TV shows (and, consequently, learn Ukrainian!)
- Study strategies to make sure you're learning lots of Ukrainian while you watch.

Which series should you choose?

The most important thing is to choose a show you really like. It's pointless choosing a drama/thriller like *The Realm* if you don't like this genre. You'll get bored and drop it in no time.

Try to think about the kind of series you get hooked on in your native language and look for something similar.

How do you choose the right show for your level?

Some shows might not be the best option depending on your level. Let's take a popular show in English as an example: *Game of Thrones*. Being an epic story, it is a pretty complicated and demanding series, especially for beginners and 'older' vocabulary is often used: words like 'jester' and 'mummer' which are practically useless at this stage. The fact that each episode lasts about an hour also makes it difficult to follow.

The best way to find out whether a Ukrainian TV show is suitable is by putting yourself to the test. Choose a show and play an episode with both the audio and Ukrainian subtitles on. Watch the episode for a few minutes.

If you can follow the Ukrainian TV show, great!

From now on, you will only watch this and other series with the Ukrainian subtitles on, listening and reading at the same time. This will help you memorize and see the usage of words you already know, and it will especially, help you understand what's being said by getting your ears used to these sounds while you read the words. If you find words or phrases you don't know, you can pause the episode and write them down or add them into a flashcard app like Anki (https://apps.ankiweb.net). Over time, this will become more and more natural, and when you feel comfortable enough, you may even abandon the Ukrainian subtitles.

If you found it was too hard to follow even with the subtitles on, don't worry; you still have some options.

You might struggle to keep up, either because:

- There are too many words you don't know.
- They speak too fast.

If you are not already aware of it, there's an amazing Chrome extension that will help. It's called Language Learning with Netflix and has interactive subtitles that you can click on to get the definition in your native language. It also pauses automatically after every line to help you keep up. Give it a try—it could transform your Ukrainian!

Using a Ukrainian TV show as a study resource

If you find Ukrainian TV shows hard to follow even with the sub-titles on, then start with a learner series.

One of the reasons Ukrainian TV series can be tricky to follow is that they're designed for native speakers—people who've spent their whole lives (at least 105,120 hours for an average 18-year-old) listening to Ukrainian. No wonder they're tricky for learners!

Another option is to try using subtitles in your native language, just to get your ears more used to the new sounds.

One of the dangers with this technique is that you focus too much on reading the subtitles in your language and you don't benefit much from the Ukrainian audio.

One thing you can do to get around this is to pay as much attention to the audio as you can. You'll notice that many words and expressions are repeated quite often by the actors.

When this happens and you don't know them, write them down in your study notebook or add them into a flashcards app like Anki (https://apps.ankiweb.net/). If you can't identify the words by ear, write down what's written in the English subtitles and use a dictionary to translate it or just Google it. Alternatively, you can flip to the Ukrainian subtitles to see the expression written down

In the meantime, keep studying Ukrainian and learning more vocabulary, and over time, you'll notice that you understand more of the sentences without even reading the subtitles anymore. At this point, take the test above again to check if you can move onto the Ukrainian subtitles phase.

Activities to boost your learning with Ukrainian TV shows

Sometimes, when you're watching Ukrainian TV shows, it feels magical. You're sitting there in your sweatpants, eating ice-cream and learning Ukrainian at the same time. It's a win-win scenario.

But then a niggling doubt creeps in... Is this enough? Shouldn't I be doing more to learn Ukrainian? While watching Ukrainian TV can do a lot for your listening and speaking, there are more focused activities you can do to accelerate your learning.

The best bit—they still involve watching some TV!

The reality is that TV and films help you speak naturally and understand more.

If you spend all of your time just learning the slow and stilted dialogues that you find in textbooks, you'll probably end up speaking in a slow and stilted way.

Alternatively, if you listen to lots of realistic conversations in TV series and films, over time, you'll start speaking in a more natural way.

The same goes for understanding: if you only listen to learner materials, you'll get used to hearing a version of the language that's been watered down for foreigners. You might get a shock when you hear people using it in real life!

On the flip side, if you get used to hearing realistic dialogues in TV series and films (even if it's tricky at first!), you'll be much better equipped to follow conversations in the real world.

I'm not suggesting you try to learn a language entirely by watching TV and films. Learner materials like textbooks and audio courses have their place in a language learner's toolkit. And as previously stated, speaking practice is essential to perfecting Ukrainian.

Foreign-language TV series and films are like handy supplements that can help you bridge the gap between learner materials and how people actually talk.

What if I don't understand anything?

When people think of learning a language by watching TV, they sometimes imagine learning through something akin to osmosis—the idea that if you listen to a stream of undecipherable syllables for long enough, it will eventually start to make some sort of sense.

But it doesn't work like that.

To learn, you first have to understand the language. Once you get to a high(ish) level where you can pick out a fair amount of what the characters are saying, you can learn a lot from just sitting back and listening.

What if you're not there yet?

Before that, if you want to learn a language by watching TV and films, it's important to do activities that'll help you understand the dialogues. The following activities will help you do just that.

How to learn a language by watching TV and films: what you'll need

First, you'll need a film, TV series, or YouTube video with two sets of subtitles: one in the language you're learning and one in your native language. This used to be tricky, but with YouTube, Netflix, Amazon, Hulu and Apple it's getting easier and easier to find videos that are subtitled in multiple languages. Aim for videos where people speak in a modern and natural way (i.e., no period dramas).

One of the best of these is *Easy Ukrainian* on YouTube. The presenters interview people on the street, so you get used to hearing natives speak in a natural and spontaneous way. What's more, the videos are subtitled both in the target language and in English.

If you're a beginner and you find these kinds of videos overwhelming (too many new words and grammar points), they also have a "super easy" series that you can use to get started.

Write what you hear

One super task to boost your listening skills is to use the videos as a dictation:

- Listen to very small pieces of the video (a few seconds each) and write down what you hear.
- Listen several times until you can't pick out any more.
- Compare what you wrote against the subtitles.
- Look up new words in a dictionary and write them down so you can review them later.

Often you'll see words and phrases that you understand on the page but couldn't pick out in the listening. You can now focus on the difference between how words are written and how people actually say them in real life.

This is your chance to become an expert at listening.

Make it your mission to become aware of these differences. Do speakers squash certain words together? Do they cut out some sounds or words completely? You may notice some things that native speakers have never realized about their own language and that teachers won't teach you.

Here is an example:

- In spoken English, "do you" often sounds like "dew," and "want" sounds like "one." So the phrase "do you want it" is pronounced like "dew one it."

No wonder listening is trickier than reading!

An awareness of these differences is your new secret weapon for understanding fast speech and developing a natural speaking style: the more you pay attention to these differences, the better you'll get at speaking and listening to the language as it's used in real life.

Translate it

Another invaluable task is to translate small passages into your native language and back into the language you're learning. After you've done this, you can check what you wrote in your target language against the original subtitles.

Ideally, you should translate the passage into your native language one day and back into your target language the day after so that you have to use your existing knowledge about grammar and vocabulary to recreate the dialogue (rather than just relying on memory).

This technique works because it gives you the chance to practice creating sentences in your target language and then compare them against the sentences of native speakers. In this way, you'll be able to see the gap between how you use the language and how the experts (the native speakers) do it. This will help you learn to express ideas and concepts like they do.

Comparing your performance to the experts' and taking steps to close the gap is a key element of deliberate practice, a powerful way to master new skills that is supported by decades of research.

Get into character.

One fun way to learn a language from TV and films is to learn a character's part from a short scene. Choose a character you like and pretend to be them. Learn their lines and mimic their pronunciation as closely as possible. You can even try to copy their body language. This is a great method for a couple of reasons:

- It's an entertaining way to memorize vocabulary and grammar structures.
- By pretending to be a native speaker, you start to feel like one – it's a fun way to immerse yourself in the culture.

If you are really up for it, record yourself and compare it to the original. Once you get over the cringe factor of seeing yourself on video or hearing your own voice, you'll be able to spot some differences between yourself and the original, which will give you valuable insight into the areas you need to improve. For example: does your "r" sound very different to theirs? Did you forget a word or grammar point?

Talk about it

A great way to improve your speaking skills is the key word method:

- As you watch a scene, write down key words or new vocabulary
- Once you've finished watching, look at your list of words and use them as prompts to speak aloud for a few minutes about what you just saw.

As well as helping you practice your speaking skills, this method gives you the chance to use the new words you just learned, which will help you remember them more easily in the future.

Just relax and chill out

If you're feeling tired or overstretched and the previous four steps feel too much like hard work, you can use films and TV as a non-strenuous way to keep up your language learning routine. Get yourself a nice hot drink, make yourself comfortable on the sofa, put on a film or TV series and try to follow what's going on. Even if most of it washes over you, it's better than nothing.

While you obviously can't learn a language entirely by doing this, it's still handy because it helps you build the following four skills:

- Get used to trying to understand what's going on even if there's lots of ambiguity and you only understand the odd word (a useful skill to develop for real-life conversations!).
- Get your ears used to the intonation and sounds of the language.
- Become familiar with words and expressions that are repeated a lot.
- Stay in your language routine during times when you can't be bothered to study.

Don't underestimate the value of this last point: if you skip language learning completely during periods when you're tired or busy, you'll get out of the routine and probably end up feeling guilty. As time passes, it'll get harder and harder to get started again. But if you keep it up on those days, even by just watching a few minutes of something on the sofa, you'll stay in the routine and find it easy to put in more effort once you get your time and energy back.

CHAPTER TEN

NAVIGATING THE RESTAURANT

Who doesn't love to eat?

Explore delicious local foods while abroad—you won't be sorry! Or if you are very, very lucky, go to a Ukrainian restaurant in your home town, (you are more likely to have success searching out general Slavic or Russian cuisine though!).

Spending time at restaurants or bars can really factor into your cultural immersion and Ukrainian-language-learning experience.

Access to a fully equipped kitchen can be hard to come by while traveling, and you may well prefer to dedicate your time to seeing the sights rather than grocery shopping (though I'll be the first to tell you that exploring a local market can be extremely fun). Talk to locals, find out where the hot spots are, and ask about regional cuisine. People love to talk about food as much as they love to eat it!

No plans to travel? Join in on the fun by visiting a Ukrainian bar/restaurant with Ukrainian-speaking staff. They might be hard to find, but there are some about.

You may be worried about your pronunciation, especially if you are not familiar with phonetic spelling. Don't worry; there are a ton of resources online that can help you hear and speak Ukrainian words. They are mentioned throughout the book, in the bibliography, and at the end. Use them and practice out loud as much as possible.

Ukrainian cuisine

"What should I eat in the Ukraine?" Is one of the first things people ask, even before "What should I do?" or "Where should I stay?" in Kyiv.

But what exactly is Ukrainian food?

What is Ukrainian cuisine?

Ukrainian national cuisine developed in its main features in the early XIX century, and finally took shape in the first half of XX century. Ukrainian cuisine combines great amount of various regional customs. Furthermore, the Polish, Hungarian, Germanic, Turkish, Tatar and Russian culinary traditions had a notable influence on the uniqueness of its recipes.

During its existence, Ukrainian cuisine has come long and interesting path from simple to complex dishes, which have very interesting ways of cooking. Gradually developing, being in close proximity with other nations and with their culinary tastes, the Ukrainians have created their own unique set of products and methods of preparation.

There are thousands of national dishes. Some of them may seem extraordinary because of the unusual combinations. Nevertheless you will be surprised by the unique taste which they create.

The centerpiece of Ukrainian cuisine is bread which is made from rye or wheat flour and baked in the traditional oven.

Salo—is a favourite national product. It is served not only as a separate dish (salted, boiled, smoked and fried), but also as a condiment and fat base for a great variety of dishes, even sweet, combining it with sugar or syrup.

Vegetables play an important role in Ukrainian cuisine. Beetroot stands on the first place and it can be called a national vegetable. Other vegetables such as carrot, pumpkin, potatoes, tomatoes and corn, which are also very popular in Ukraine.

There are a lot of recipes containing cherry, plum, pear, currant and watermelon, as these fruits and berries are some of the favorites in Ukraine.

Traditional Ukrainian dishes:

Borsch

Every tourist who visits Ukraine wants to taste this dish. In fact, it's no wonder since this soup is cooked by Ukrainian families very often and Ukrainians are experts in borsch. According to a survey of Ukrainians, borsch is the favorite food of the whole nation.

Holubsti

This traditional dish is adored by many Ukrainians. It is usually cooked by stuffing cabbage leaves with minced meat and rice and then stewing them in tomato sauce. However, the classic recipe for cabbage rolls often varies depending on the region. However, this does not in any way make the recipes for this delicious and nutritious meal less traditional.

Kholodets

This is a unique cold dish which Ukrainians cook both as an everyday or as a festive meal. In short, kholodets is a jellied meat broth that includes pieces of meat and sometimes vegetables. There are also recipes for a fish jelly made with fish and fish broth. So kholodets is a traditional Ukrainian appetizers that resembles salted jelly and can be eaten alone or served with mustard/horseradish.

Varenyky

Varenyky are traditional Ukrainian dumplings filled with a variety of ingredients. They can be sweet (with sour cherries, guelder roseberries, strawberries, cheese, jam, etc) or salty (with potatoes, mushrooms, meat, cracklings, cabbage, salty cheese, etc).

Nalysnyky

Nalysnyky are a delicate traditional dish cooked using egg batter and diverse fillings. It is cooked in two stages: first, the pancakes are fried and then they are filled with the stuffing which is usually made in advance. Pancakes also are symbols of Masliana (Cheese Week) and they are cooked everyday during the holiday season. But Ukrainians have come to love them so much that they cook nalysnyky for breakfast, dinner and even serve them during other holidays.

Syrnyky

Syrnyk is a sweet pancake made with farmer's cheese, flour, eggs and sugar. This is a delicious, healthy and sweet dish that can be served at breakfast for a large family.

Vocabulary and phrases for the restaurant

English	Ukrainian	Pronunciation (stress underlined)
bread (Sg)	хліб	khib
breads (P)	хліби́	khlibý
roll (Sg)	булка	bulka
rolls (P)	булки	bulky
butter	масло	masio
cheese	сир	syr
honey	мед	med
jam	варення	varennya
egg (Sg)	яйцо	yaitso
eggs (P)	яйця	yaitsia
noodles	спагеті	spaheti
rice	риз	ryz

yoghurt (*Sg*)	йогурт	yohurt
yoghurts (*Pg*)	йогурти	yohurty
sugar	цукор	tsukor
salt	сіль	sil'
pepper	перець	perets'
spice	спеці	spetsi
oil	масло	masio
(to) eat	їсти	yisty
food	харчування	kharchuvannya
(to) drink	пити	pyty
drink (*Sg*)	напій	napiy
drinks (*Pl*)	напої	napoyi
hungry	голоден	holoden (*m*)
	голодна	holodna (*f*)
thirsty	жаждучій	zhazhduchiy
(to) cook	готувати	hotuvaty
delicious	смачний	smachnyy
cheers!	Будьмо!	budmo!
breakfast	сніданкя	snidannya
lunch	обід	obid
dinner	навечеря	navecherya
restaurant (*Sg*)	ресторан	restoran
restaurants (*Pl*)	ресторани	restorany
bar (*Sg*)	бар	bar
bars (*Pl*)	бари	bary
café	кафе	kafe
soup (*Sg*)	суп	sup
soups (*Pl*)	супи	supy
salad (*Sg*)	салат	salat
salads (*Pl*)	салати	salaty

french fries	фрікти	frikty
cutlery	прибори	prybory
fork	вилка	vylka
spoon	ложка	lozhka
knife	ніж	nizh
plate	тарілка	tarilka
glass	стакан	stakan
cup	чаша	chasha
mug	крожка	krozhka
water	вода	voda
sparkling water	газирівка	hazyrivka
still water	тиха вода	tykha voda
juice (*Sg*)	сік	sik
juices (*Pl*)	соки	soky
beer	пиво	pyvo
wine	вино	vyno
champagne	шампанське	shampans'ke
cocktail	коктейл	koktell
milk	молоко	moloko
cocoa	какао	kakao
coffee	кава	kava
tea	чай	chai
sweet	солодкий	solodkyy
sour	кислий	kyslyy
spicy	гострій	hostriy
salty	солоний	solonyy
bitter	гіркий	hirkyy
fruit	фрукти	frukty
vegetables	овочі	ovochi
apple (*Sg*)	яблука	yabluka

apples (*Pl*)	яблуки	yabluky
orange (*Sg*)	апельсіна	apel'sina
oranges (*Pl*)	апелдсіни	apel'siny
strawberry (*Sg*)	клубник	klubnyk
strawberries (*Pl*)	клубники	klubnyky
banana (*Sg*)	банана	banana
bananas (*Pl*)	банани	banany
potato (*Sg*)	бульба	bul'ba
potatoes (*Pl*)	бульби	bul'by
cucumber (*Sg*)	агурчік	ahurchik
cucumbers (*Pl*)	агурчіки	ahurchiky
meat	м'ясо	m'yaso
sausage (*Sg*)	ковбаса	kovbasa
sausages (*Pl*)	ковбаси	kovbasy
ham	вітчина	vitchyna
chicken	куриця	kurytsia
fish	риба	ryba
beef	гов'ядина	hov'yadyna
lamb	бараніна	baranina
chocolate	шоколад	shokolad
pie (*Sg*)	торт	tort
pies (*Pl*)	торти	torty
cake (*Sg*)	торт	tort
cakes (*Pl*)	торти	torty
biscuit	печення	pechennya
ice cream	морозиво	morozyvo

Phrases for drinking and dining in Ukrainian

I would like a salad	Я хочу замовити салат

Could I have a draft beer, please?	Принесіть, будь ласка, кегове пиво.
What time do you stop serving?	До якої години ви працюєте?
Is this table free?	Цей столик вільний?
Could I have the check, please?	Чи можу я отримати чек?
When you can, please.	Коли завгодно
What do I owe?	Скільки я вам винен?
Do we need a reservation?	Чи потрібно нам замовляти столик?
Could we make a reservation?	Чи можемо ми замовити столик?
I have a reservation	Я замовляв столик
Could we see the menu, please?	Принесіть, будь ласка, меню.
Could I have a glass of tap water?	Принесіть, будь ласка, склянку звичайної води.
I would like my steak medium rare	Я хотів би стейк слабкої просмажки
This dish is too salty	Ця страва занадто солона
Are there seats available outside?	Чи є вільні місця на вулиці?
How large is the portion?	На скільки великі порції?
How much is a glass of red wine?	Скільки коштує склянка червоного вина?
Can I pay by debit card?	Чи можу я заплатити дебетовою карткою?
Do you take Mastercard here?	Ви приймаєте MasterCard?

Does this dish have gluten?	Ця страва містить клейковину?
I am allergic to nuts	У мене алергія на горіхи
Do you have a kid's menu?	Чи є у вас є дитяче меню?
Do you have a highchair?	Чи є у вас є високий дитячий стілець?
What do you have for dessert?	Що у вас є на десерт?
Can we order this to go?	Чи можемо ми замовити це, щоб з'їсти вдома?
Could you please bring me a spoon.	Будь ласка, передай мені ложку.
Where are the restrooms?	Де знаходиться туалет?
Enjoy your meal!	Смачного!
What can I get you?	Що я можу вам запропонувати?
I am lactose intolerant	У мене непереносимість лактози.
We need a table for four	Нам треба столик на чотирьох (*Nam tryeba stolik na chotirʲokh*)
I would like to reserve a table for two	Я хотів би замовити столик на двох (*Ya khotiv bi zamoviti stolik na dvokh*)
What do you recomment?	Що б ви порадили? (*Shto b vi poradili*)
What is included?	Що включено? (Shto vklyochyeno)

Does it come with a salad?	Чи страва разом із салатом? (*Chi strava razom iz salatom*)
What is the soup of the day?	Який сьогодні суп дня? (*Yakiy sʲoguodni soop dnya*)
What are today's specials?	Які сьогодні знижки? (*Yaki sʲoguodni znizki*)
What would you like to eat?	Що б ви бажали замовити поїсти? (*Shto b vi baẓali zamoviti poyisti*)
The dessert of the day	Десерт дня (*Dyesyert dnya*)
I would like to try the regional dish	Я хотів би спробувати місцеву страву (*Ya khotiv bi sproboovati mistzyevoo stravoo*)
What type of meat do you have?	Який вид м'яса у вас є? (*Yakiy vid m'yasa oo vas ye*)
I need a napkin	Мені потрібна серветка (*Myeni potribna syervyetka*)
Can you give me some more water?	Не могли б ви принести ще? (*Nye moguli b vi prinyesti shtye*)
Can you pass me the salt?	Чи не могли б ви передати сіль? (*Chi nye moguli b vi pyeryedati silʲ*)
Can you bring me fruit?	Не могли б ви принести мені фрукти?

	(*Nye moguli b vi prinyesti myeni frookti*)
Hot dog	Хот-дог (*Khot-dogu*)
Hamburger	Гамбургер (*Guamboorguyer*)
Steak	Стейк (*Styeyk*)
Sandwich	Бутерброд (*Bootyerbrod*)
A portion	Частина (*Chastina*)
A little more	Трохи більше (*Trokhi bilʲshye*)
More	Більше (*Bilʲshye*)
A little	Трохи (*Trokhi*)
Too much	Занадто (*Zanadto*)
Receipt	Квитанція (*Kvitantziya*)
Can I pay with a credit card?	Чи можу я сплатити кредитною карткою? (*Chi moʒoo ya splatiti kryeditnoyo kartkoyo*)
The bill, please	Рахунок, будь ласка (*Rakhoonok, boodʲ laska*)
Do you have another credit card?	У вас є інша кредитна картка?

	(*Oo vas ye insha kryeditna kartka*)
Do you accept credit cards?	Ви приймаєте кредитні картки? (*Vi priymayetye kryeditni kartki*)
I need a receipt	Мені потрібна квитанція (*Myeni potribna kvitantziya*)
How much do I owe you?	Скільки я вам винен? (*Skilʲki ya vam vinyen*)
I am going to pay with cash	Я збираюся платити готівкою (*Ya zbirayosya platiti guotivkoyo*)
Thank you for the good service	Дякую вам за гарне обслуговування (*Dyakooyo vam za guarnye obslooguovoovannya*)
Can I speak with the manager?	Можу я поговорити з менеджером? (*Moʐoo ya poguovoriti z myenyedʐyerom*)
The food is cold	Їжа холодна (*Yiʐa kholodna*)
It is cold	Це холодне (*Tzye kholodnye*)
Is it spicy?	Чи це гостра страва? (*Chi tzye guostra strava*)
This is burnt	Пережарений (*Pyeryeʐaryeniy*)

This is dirty	Брудний
	(*Broodniy*)
I do not want pepper	Я не хочу перець
	(*Ya nye khochoo pyeryetzʲ*)
I do not like beans	Я не люблю квасолю
	(*Ya nye lyoblyo kvasolyo*)
I do not like garlic	Я не люблю часник
	(Ya nye lyoblyo chasnik)

About Ukrainian food

As a country known to be the breadbasket of Europe, Ukraine has an abundance of good quality foods at reasonable prices. A large portion of food consumed in Ukraine is grown naturally by small farmers and is mostly organic. Because of the natural farming methods used, food in the Ukraine has a lot of flavors and a fresh natural taste. In the Ukraine, many people prefer to buy food at farmers' markets where prices are lower and food quality better compared to western-style supermarkets. Many tourists to the Ukraine rediscover the long-forgotten taste of freshly picked strawberries, tomatoes, cucumbers and other fruit and vegetables grown in open fields and harvested in season.

Restaurants in the Ukraine

While consumer goods in Ukraine cost the same or more compared to Western countries, food in Ukraine costs less. A wide variety of restaurants and cafes has sprung up in Ukrainian cities in the recent years. In cities such as Lviv, you will find many eating places serving excellent food. Food can also be bought from many small grocery stores, some of which are open 24 hours. In rural towns and in villages in the Ukraine, restaurants are rare but grocery stores are everywhere. Most of the restaurants in Lviv and Kyiv have menus in English and Ukrainian..

Eating Out in Ukraine

The restaurants in Kiev are remarkably diverse. In addition to Ukrainian cuisine, there are many others (Asian, Mediterranean, American, and Georgian) that provide the opportunity for everyone to find the best choice to suit their personal tastes. If you are going to Kiev, just give the Ukrainian capital a chance to surprise you with the cooking of some of the following restaurants:

Kanapa

Located on Andrew's Descent, one of Kiev's most famous streets, Kanapa perfectly reflects the area's historic and creative significance by serving modern reinterpretations of traditional Eastern European dishes like caviar and beetroot soup. Kanapa is a restaurant reminiscent of the literary salons of the 19th century: your meal may be accompanied by chamber music or a book reading, and all the artwork on the walls is for sale. In the summer, guests can enjoy a moment of peace on the terrace overlooking a wooded area.

Imbir

Vegetarian food and the relaxing atmosphere of a library or bookstore is what you'll find at Imbir. One of the only restaurants in the city to provide a completely vegetarian menu, it is full of books and comfortable armchairs, a sure way to make visitors want to stay there for hours on end. With a very reasonably priced lunch menu that changes every day, it's an ideal spot for tourists and regulars alike. Their drinks are as healthy as their food: different sorts of tea and fresh fruit juice, and also almond milk drinks and detox smoothies.

Shoti

Anyone in Eastern Europe should take advantage of the opportunity to sample food from the Caucasus, not so common in the rest of the world. Shoti, a Georgian restaurant, is just the place for such a discovery. Its exquisitely designed award-winning interior and summer terrace make it a very attractive location, but it's not just a pretty place without substance. You'll also find some quintessentially Georgian dishes such as pork and veal *khinkali* (dumplings) and a type of cheese-filled bread known as *khachapuri*.

Tsarske Selo

Right opposite the world-famous Pechersk Lavra monastery, Tsarske Selo is popular with tourists and travelers looking for genuine Ukrainian cuisine as they take a break from sightseeing. The interior is a recreation of a typical 17th-century house in a Ukrainian village, and food is prepared following traditional recipes and methods. Tsarske Selo is perfect if you are looking for a place to eat after having visited the monastery and would like to extend your discovery of Ukraine's history and folklore while eating.

CHAPTER ELEVEN

PARTYING

You're in Kiev, and you've decided to sample the nightlife. From bog-standard boozers to elite cocktail joints, from classy casinos to scintalliting strip clubs, from underground rock venues to hands-in-the-air house havens, Kiev has got a bit of everything and whichever nightspot you happen to visit, it's normally going off at a hundred miles an hour.

If you're more of a bar lizard than club fiend, then you may want to start the night in either one of Kiev's popular Irish pubs. **O'Briens** is a good bet for the genuine pub atmosphere, whilst **Golden Gate** is a bit more upmarket. For those however who couldn't think of anything worse than coming all the way to Kiev only to find themselves listening to a whacky Paddy talking crap about Leprechauns or some such rubbish, then go authentic Ukrainian at one of Kiev's finest beer taverns. **Shato** and **Viola's Bierstube** both serve excellent brews in a fun and friendly environs. Meanwhile cool cats will want to head for **Antresol** and **Babuin** to hang out with fellow artistic types and get the lowdown on the murky world of Ukrainian politics. Live music aficionados meanwhile should head to **Dockers** for a heady mix of rock and vodka.

Once you've got a few beers and vodkas under your belt, it's time to explore Kiev's nightlife proper. Kiev's nightclubs take some seeing to be believed thanks to their raucous atmosphere and full on hedonism

If you fancy seeing them for yourself then put on your smartest gear and head down to the likes of Faberge, Decadence House or Arena. An excellent option for those that fancy something slightly less pretentious is **PaTiPa**.

Finally, if you're lucky enough to be in Kyiv in sweltering summer then a night at **Privilege** is a must. Yes, the same *Privilege* that has the cool kids of Ibiza in a spin has it's own branch in Kiev. An open air party under the stars, just by the Dynamo Kiev stadium. Unforgettable!

A close rival to Kiev and its nightlife is Odesa. It is not by chance that Odessa has become the most popular Ukrainian resort city, because there is not only the sea and excellent beaches, but also entertainment for every taste. This city never sleeps—every night all year round Odessa dances and has fun in numerous Odesa Night Clubs that offer rest for any budget and preferences. Odessa Nightlife is truly diverse: beach clubs with bright night parties by the sea, closed clubs with pretentious VIP parties for the elite visitors, art cafes, karaoke, restaurants and bars that work around the clock, and those where you can not only have a tasty meal and drink in a fun company, but also dance or listen to concerts of rock, folk and jazz music.

Ministerium Club located in the city center is the most expensive and pretentious in Odessa. Ministerium is a very beautiful mansion with a restaurant, karaoke bar, lounge area and several concert halls, where very special and bright parties take place every evening. In the summer, Ministerium offers cozy summer terrace with a superb view of the center of Odessa and pleasant live music.

Among tourists and guests of the city, **Ibiza Beach Club**, which is open from May to September, is the most popular nightclub. Every night in Ibiza you can dance until dawn with the best music right by the sea, and relax in the lounge area near the pools. Ibiza is one of the most popular concert venues in the city, where world pop stars regularly perform.

Ithaka Night and Beach Club, located in Arcadia, is no less popular. This club is stylized as an ancient Hellas, has a bar area with the widest choice of various cocktails, a night club with the best Odessa DJs, a restaurant with Mediterranean and European cuisine, and a large concert arena.

Plyazhnik Nightclub is not the most famous Odessa venue, but it has its constant clientele. This institution has strict face control. Entry is allowed only to those who have reached 21 years old and at the same time has a decent appearance.

Those who like disco of the 80s-90s will not be bored in Odessa either, because there is **Praetoria Nightclub** specializing in thematic dance parties of that time. Experienced DJs mix well-known hits so that no one can sit still.

If you are not a fan of dancing, but you like to eat tasty food in a cozy atmosphere and sing your favorite songs, go to **Opera Prestige**—24\7 karaoke restaurant. This is one of the best karaoke in Odessa—thanks to professional equipment and experienced sound engineers, every performer can feel like a real star here.

In the center of Odessa there is excellent art-cafe **Wardrobe**; it has low prices for food and drinks, and every evening guests are entertained by a variety of musical groups, performing songs and music of various genres.

Some useful phrases when sampling the nightlife:

What time do you stop serving?	До якої години ви працюєте?
Could I have a draft beer, please?	Принесіть, будь ласка, кегове пиво.
Is this table free?	Цей столик вільний?
When you can, please.	Коли завгодно
What do I owe?	Скільки я вам винен?
Could we make a reservation?	Чи можемо ми замовити столик?
I have a reservation	Я замовляв столик
Where are the restrooms?	Де знаходиться туалет?
What can I get you?	Що я можу вам запропонувати?
What's your name?	Як тебе звати?
It's nice to meet you	Дуже приємно

	познайомитись
Where are you from?	Звідки ти?
What do you do?	Чим ти займаєшся?
What do you like to do for fun?	Як ти розважаєшся?
Do you come here often?	Як часто ти тут буваєш?
I'm here on vacation	Я тут у відпустці
Your work sounds interesting	У тебе цікава робота
You're so funny	Ти такий кумедний
You're really cute	Ти дуже милий
Are you here alone?	Ти тут один?
Do you have a boyfriend?	У тебе є хлопець?
Do you have a girlfriend?	У тебе є дівчина?
I'm so lucky to have met you	Мені пощастило познайомитися з тобою
I like you a lot	Ти мені дуже подобаєшся
I love your smile	Я люблю твою усмішку
Can I buy you a drink?	Чи можна пригостити тебе напоєм?
What would you like to have?	Що би ти хотіла?
Let me get this round	Покладись на мене
Do you dance?	Ти танцюєш?
Can I see you again?	Чи зможу я тебе знову побачити?
Would you like to go out for dinner some time?	Може повечеряємо колись разом?
Do you want to get out of here?	Може підемо в якесь інше місце?
Would you like to meet me for coffee?	Може зустрінемося за горнятком кави?

Thanks for a great conversation	Дякую за чудову розмову
I'm glad I came here tonight	Радий, що прийшов сюди сьогодні
I had a great time with you tonight	Я добре провів цей вечір із тобою
rum	ром
whisky	віскі
sparkling white wine	ігристе вино
champagne	шампанське
brandy	бренді
port wine	портвейн
cocktail	коктейль
shot	рюмка
wine	вино
soft drink	освіжаючий напій

CHAPTER TWELVE

TRAVEL

You've bought your ticket, your bags are packed, and you can't wait to begin your journey to the Ukraine.

Now, there is a simple thing you can do that can have a very big impact on your trip.

Learn some Ukrainian travel phrases!

Your trip will be so much more fun and meaningful if you can communicate with locals.

Below are the bare essentials, the most common survival Ukrainian travel phrases and words you will need on your trip.

Useful Ukrainian travel phrases every traveler should learn

Before you move beyond greetings, here is a tip for learning the words and phrases in this chapter: The best way to study them is to hear them in use. So place special attention to when people greet each other in TV series or films.

Ukrainian greetings

Ukrainians are generally very polite, and you must always be courteous and say, "Hello" and "How are you?"

Do not worry about making mistakes; most people will try their utmost to understand you and to make sure you understand them. Just try your best, and they will be happy to reciprocate. Some of the phrases you will be already familiar with from earlier on in this book but there is no harm in revision (or to put it more plainly repetition)!

Essential short phrases:

Greetings

English	Ukrainian	Pronunciation
Hello!	Привіт!	pry-vIt
Greetings!	Вітаю!	vi-tA-ju
Good morning!	Доброго ранку	dO-bro-ho rAn-ku
Good afternoon!	Доброго дня!	dO-bro-ho dnja
Good evening!	Доброго вечора!	dO-bro-ho vE-cho-ra
How are you doing?	Як ся маєш?	jak sjA mA-jesh
How are you?	Як справи?	jak sprA-vy
I'm fine, thanks!	Добре, дякую!	dO-bre, djA-ku-ju
And you?	А в тебе?	a v tE-be
So-so	Не дуже	ne dU-zhe

Getting to know people

English	Ukrainian	Pronunciation
Let me introduce myself	Дозвольте представитися	*do-zvOl'-te predstA-vy-ty-sja*
My name is...	Мене звати…	*me-nE zvA-ty*
What is your name?	Як тебе звати?	*jak te-bE zvA-ty*
Nice to meet you!	Радий познайомитися!	*rA-dyj po-zna-jO-my-ty-sja*
I'm from...	Я з…	*ja z…*
Where are you from?	Звідки ти?	*zvI-dky tY*
How old are you?	Скільки тобі років?	*skIL'-ky to-bI rO-kiv*
I am 25	Мені 25 років	*me-nI 25 rO-kiv*
Where do you live?	Де ти живеш?	*dE tY zhy-vEsh*
Nice to meet you!	Дуже приємно!	*dU-zhe pry-jEm-no*
I am a foreigner	Я іноземець	*ja i-no-zE-mets'*

Question words

English	Ukrainian	Pronunciation
Who?	Хто…?	*khto*
What?	Що…?	*scho*
When?	Коли…?	*ko-LY*
Which?	Який…? (mas) Яка…? (fem)	*ja-kY* *ja-kA*

Where?	Де…?	*de*
How?	Як…?	*jak*
Why?	Чому…?	*cho-mU*
How much?	Скільки…?	*skIL'-ky*

Getting around

English	Ukrainian	Pronunciation
Street	Вулиця	*vU-ly-tsja*
Railway station	Вокзал	*vok-zAL*
Post office	Пошта	*pO-shta*
Cafe	Кафе	*ka-fE*
Restaurant	Ресторан	*re-sto-rAn*
Market	Ринок	*rY-nok*
Supermarket	Супермаркет	*su-per-mAr-ket*
Museum	Музей	*mu-zEj*
Hospital	Лікарня	*li-kAr-nja*
Metro	Метро	*me-trO*
Bus	Автобус	*av-tO-bus*
Tramway	Трамвай	*tram-vAj*
Taxi	Таксі	*ta-ksI*

Directions

English	Ukrainian	Pronunciation
Where is it?	Де це?	*dE tse*
Is it far from here?	Це далеко?	*tse da-LE-ko*
Is it this or that way?	Туди чи сюди?	*tu-dY chy sju-dY*
Which side...	В яку сторону…	*v jakU stO-ro-nu*

How to go to...	Як пройти до…	*jak proj-tY do*

Asking for help

English	Ukrainian	Pronunciation
Do you need help?	Вам допомогти?	*vam do-po-moh-tY*
Help me please	Допоможіть мені, будь ласка	*do-po-mo-zhIt' me-nI bud' LAs-ka*
What time is it?	Котра година?	*kot-rA ho-dY-na*
Allow me...	Дозвольте…	*doz-vOL'-te*
May I...	Чи можу я…?	*chy mO-zhu ja*
I don't speak understand you	Я вас не розумію	*ja vas ne ro-zu-mI-ju*
Do you understand me?	Ви розумієте мене?	*vy ro-zu-mI-je-te me-nE*
I don't know	Я не знаю	*ja ne znA-ju*
Could you repeat, please?	Повторіть, будь ласка!	*pov-to-rIt' bud' LAs-ka*
I'm lost	Я заблукав	*ja za-blu-kAv*
I don't speak Ukrainian	Я не розмовляю українською	*a ne ro-zmov-ljA-ju uk-ra-jIns'-ko-ju*
What's that?	Що це?	*scho tse*
What does it mean?	Що це означає?	*scho tse o-zna-chA-je*
Could you speak slower?	Говоріть повільніше, будь ласка	*ho-vo-rIt' po-vil'-nI-she bud' LAs-ka*
Do you speak English?	Ви говорите англійською?	*vy ho-vO-ry-te anh-LIjs'-ko-ju*
How can I go	Як туди пройти?	*jak tu-dY pro-jtY*

there?		
Are you okay?	Що з вами?	*scho z vA-my?*
What do you want?	Що ви хочете?	*scho vy khO-che-te*
How much does it cost?	Скільки це коштує?	*skIL'-ky tse kOsh-tu-je*

Being polite

English	Ukrainian	Pronunciation
Thank you!	Дякую!	*djA-ku-ju*
Thank you very much!	Дуже дякую!	*du-zhe djA-ku-ju*
You are welcome!	Будь ласка!	*bud' LAs-ka*
My pleasure!	Нема за що!	*ne-mA za scho*
Excuse me...	Перепрошую...	*pe-re-prO-shu-ju*
I'm sorry!	Вибачте!	*vy-bach-te*
Nevermind	Нічого	*ni-chO-ho*
Don't worry	Не переживай	*ne pe-re-zhy-vAj*
I understand	Я розумію	*ja ro-zu-mI-ju*
It's okay	Все гаразд	*vse ha-rAzd*
Well done!	Молодець!	*mo-lo-dEts'*
Congratulations!	Вітаю!	*vi-tA-ju*

Emotions

English	Ukrainian	Pronunciation
I love you	Я кохаю тебе!	*ja ko-khA-ju te-bE*
Wow!	Овва!	*Ov-va*
Unfortunately...	На жаль…	*na zhAl'*

It's a pity	Шкода	*shko-dA*
Hey!	Агов!	*a-hOv*
Damn it...	Хай йому грець…	*khAj jo-mU hrets'*
What the hell?	Якого дідька?	*ja-kO-ho dId'-ka*

Saying goodbye

English	Ukrainian	Pronunciation
Bye!	Бувай	*bu-vAj*
See ya!	Па-па!	*pa-pA*
See you tomorrow!	До завтра!	*do zAv-tra*
See you soon!	До зустрічі!	*do zU-stri-chi*
Goodbye!	До побачення!	*do po-bA-chen-nja*
All the best!	Всього найкращого!	*vs'o-hO na-jkrA-scho-ho*
Take care!	Будьте здорові!	*bUd'-te zdo-rO-vi*
Have a nice evening!	Гарного вечора!	*hAr-no-ho vE-cho-ra*

Useful idioms

Як кіт наплакав   *(jak kit na-pLA-kav)*

Literally: Like a cat cried

Meaning: A drop in the ocean

Кіт в мішку   *(kit v mish-kU)*

Literally: A cat in a bag

Meaning: A pig in a poke

Собаку з'їсти *(so-bA-ku zjIs-ty)*

Literally: To eat a dog at something

Meaning: To be a dab hand at something

Вбити двох зайців одним пострілом *(vbY-ty dvokh zAj-tsiv od-nYm pO-stri-lom)*

Literally: Kill two hares with one shot

Meaning: Kill two birds with one stone

Перший хлопець на селі *(per-shyj khlo-pets' na se-LI)*

Literally: The first guy in a village

Meaning: A big frog (fish) in a little pond

Як корова на льоду *(jak ko-rO-va na l'o-dU)*

Literally: Like a cow on an ice

Meaning: Like a bull in a china shop

Спокійний як удав *(spo-kIj-nyj jak u-dAv)*

Literally: As calm as a boa

Meaning: As cool as a cucumber

Even if you can't have a fluent conversation, native Ukrainian speakers always appreciate when foreigners put the effort into learning a bit of their language. It shows respect and demonstrates that you truly want to reach out and connect with people while abroad.

You won't be totally reliant on your Ukrainian phrasebook. Yes, your Lonely Planet Ukrainian phrasebook has glossy pages and you love getting the chance to use it—but you want to be able to respond quickly when people speak to you, at a moment's notice. After learning the Ukrainian travel phrases above, you'll only need your Ukrainian phrasebook in a real pinch.

If you can express yourself with some basic Ukrainian phrases, you are less likely to be taken advantage of by taxi drivers, souvenir shops and waiters!

The perception that all Ukrainian speakers speak English is simply not true. Even in the big Ukrainian cities you'll find loads of people that know very little English. You don't want to have to track down other English speakers every time you have a question or want to make a friend.

If you want to have an edge during your upcoming travels, take a moment to memorize Ukrainian travel phrases. You won't regret it!

So there you have it: a collection of Ukrainian expressions to help you get started on your new adventure!

Practice saying everything aloud so that you will remember some of the phrases without looking and learn how to say these phrases relatively quickly and smoothly. Just hearing them spoken aloud will also help in your comprehension when people are speaking to you

Take a small pocket dictionary with you. While you don't want to try to look up verb declensions in the middle of talking with someone, you can look up nouns quickly.

Better yet, take a phrasebook. There are tons of incredible phrasebooks (some that are partially travel guides), such as those offered by Lonely Planet, that are perfect for traveling and pulling out at a moment's notice if you are really stuck. This way, if you ever forget one of your most important travel phrases, you'll be able to remind yourself

And if you find a regional Ukrainian phrasebook that focuses on your travel destination, you'll find even more useful phrases that locals love to use.

CHAPTER THIRTEEN

LEARNING LIKE A CHILD

As promised in Chapter Six, we are going to revisit what it means to *learn like a child* in greater depth.

Why is it that when we look back to our childhood, it seems that we effortlessly learned the things we truly wanted to?

There are a number of factors that we can look at individually.

- To start with, there seems to be a misinformed idea that as young adults, we have less on our minds and that this makes learning something like another language that much easier.

Mindfulness. Before you turn away in disgust and throw this book to the other side of the room shouting, "I knew it! He was a hippy all along. Now he is going to get me to cross my legs and hum OM," I am not going to ask you to do any of those things. If that is your thing, though, please feel free to do it, although I will remain dubious as to whether it will help you master another language.

I know mindfulness is a bit of a buzzword nowadays. A lot of people have heard about it but are confused about what it really means. This is not a book about mindfulness, so I am just going to go over the basics. It means focusing your awareness on the present moment and noticing your physical and emotional sensations without judgment as you are doing whatever you happen to be doing.

The benefits of mindfulness are plentiful. It increases concentration, improves self-acceptance and self-esteem, strengthens resilience, and decreases stress. In a world where we are continually subject to stress mindfulness can provide an oasis of calm.

Mindfulness (being mindful of what you do), can also help you to learn a language much more easily because a part of mindfulness involves unconscious concentration. To achieve unconscious concentration as an adult we have to practice it, unfortunately, as it is a skill many of us have lost. It is not as difficult as it sounds, and in fact, it is quite fun. Just take time out, if you get a chance, and watch some young children at play.

Look at how hard children concentrate in whatever game they are playing. They aren't making a conscious effort to concentrate; they are concentrating naturally, thoroughly immersed in the game. This is mindfulness in its most natural form, and this is what thousands of people pay hundreds of bucks every year to achieve once again.

Now, see what happens if you get one of the poor kids to stop playing and ask them to do a mundane and pre-set task like taking out the trash. Watch the child's attitude change: she's now, not just annoyed and resentful that she has been taken away from her game, but the concentration that was there when she was playing has gone. You could say her mind's not on the job, and you would be quite right. The mindfulness has gone, but it will return almost instantaneously when she resumes playing and having fun.

Games, puzzles, and challenges are all fun to us when we are young and we devote all our mind's energy to them wholeheartedly, and that is what we will try to recapture as we learn Ukrainian.

When you are actively concentrating on learning Ukrainian, it is a good idea to turn off all distractions except the method you are using to learn. By this, I mean all the gadgets we are surrounded by, such as: the telephone, radio, Facebook, Twitter, Instagram - you get the picture.

Multitasking is one of those words that is bandied about a lot nowadays - the ability to perform lots of tasks at the same time. But in this particular case, multitasking is a bad thing, a very bad thing. It has been proven that it isn't actually healthy for us and we are more efficient when we focus on just one thing at a time.

Take some deep breaths and focus all your attention on your breath. You will find your mind wandering and thoughts will distract you, but don't try to think them through or control them. Bring your attention back to your breath. It takes practice, and like learning Ukrainian, if you do it every day, you will get better at it. Also, learning to breathe better will bring more oxygen to your brain.

Before you start any learning, take a few moments to breathe and relax. If you want, do some light stretching. This allows for better blood flow before studying. Better blood flow means more oxygen to the brain—need I say more?

When it comes to studying, do the same as you did with your thoughts: if you make a mistake, do not judge yourself Instead, acknowledge it and move on. Be kind to yourself at all times. You are doing an awesome thing—be proud of it. Remember that old saying: you learn through your mistakes. It is fine to make mistakes; just remember to learn from them and not get annoyed with yourself.

Just like with being mindful, be aware of the progress you are making with your language learning, but also be patient and do not judge yourself or compare yourself with others.

If you feel like it, smile a bit (I don't mean grin like a madman) as studies have shown that smiling brings authentic feelings of well-being and reduces stress levels.

You will find your mind wandering. Everybody's mind wanders. This is fine and completely normal. Just sit back and look at the thought. Follow it but do not take part. Be an observer, as it were. You can label it if that makes it easier to dismiss, for example, "worrying," "planning," "judging," etc.

It is up to you to either act upon that and become distracted or let it go and focus on the task at hand—learning Ukrainian.

CHAPTER FOURTEEN

SPEAKING UKRAINIAN

Learning Ukrainian vs. Speaking Ukrainian

Why do you want to learn Ukrainian?

This question was put to the students learning Spanish using an app called Verbalicity (https://verbalicity.com). This is what they said:

"My wife is from Mexico, and I want to talk to her parents who don't speak a word of English."

"I'm going to Guatemala next April, and I'd like to be able to have some basic conversations with the locals."

"We get a lot of Spanish-speaking patients at the clinic where I work, and I want to communicate with them better."

What did these people have in common? They all want to learn Spanish so they can use it in the real world. In other words, they wanted to **speak Spanish.**

Nobody ever wanted to learn Ukrainian so they can stay in their house and watch Ukrainian soap operas all day.

So, if the goal is to speak Ukrainian, then why do the majority of beginners start learning Ukrainian using methods that don't actually force them to speak?

This is the single biggest mistake that most people make when learning Spanish, German, French or Ukrainian or any other language.

Most learning methods only teach you the "stuff" of Ukrainian, like the grammar, vocabulary, listening, reading, etc. Very few of them actually teach you how to speak Ukrainian.

Let's compare methods.

Methods that only teach you the "stuff" of Ukrainian:

- Apps
- Audio courses
- Group classes
- Radio/podcasts
- Reading
- Software
- Textbooks
- TV/movies

Methods that teach you to speak Ukrainian:

- Practicing with people you know
- Meetups
- Language exchanges
- Lessons with a Ukrainian teacher online or in the real world

Many language experts, like Benny Lewis, have said that studying will never help you speak a language. The best way to learn Ukrainian or any language involves more than just studying.

Let's say you are learning to drive for the first time. Your parents drop you off at the driving school for your theory class.

You spend many hours learning about traffic lights, left turns, parallel parking, and the dreaded roundabout. Your brain is filled with everything you'll ever need to know about driving a car.

Does this mean you can drive now?

No!

There's a reason why they don't give you your license right after you pass the theory test. It's because studying theory doesn't actually teach you how to drive.

You need to be behind the wheel, you need to get a "feel" for it with all of your senses, and you need to get used to making snap decisions.

Languages work in the same way.

To learn a language properly, you have to speak it.

Speaking: The one thing that makes everything else easier

You might be asking, "How am I supposed to speak if I don't learn vocabulary and grammar first?"

While it's true that a small foundation of vocabulary and grammar is necessary, the problem is that most beginners greatly overestimate how much they really need.

People spend thousands of dollars on courses and many months of self-study and still don't feel like they're "ready" to speak Ukrainian. Speaking is something that they'll put off again and again.

Scientists from the NTL Institute discovered through their research that people remember:

90% of what they learn when they use it immediately.

50% of what they learn when engaged in a group discussion.

20% of what they learn from audio-visual sources.

10% of what they learn when they've learned from reading.

5% of what they learn from lectures.

This means that the best way to learn Ukrainian is to start speaking from the beginning and try to use every new word and grammar concept in real conversations.

Speaking is the one skill that connects all the different elements of language learning. When you are speaking, you are actually improving every other aspect of the language simultaneously.

Speaking improves:

- Pronunciation
- Reading
- Writing
- Vocabulary
- Grammar
- Listening

Here's a breakdown of how speaking can improve your other language skills:

Vocabulary

Have you ever studied a word in Ukrainian but then totally drawn a blank when you tried to use it in a conversation? Well, you will. Sorry.

This happens all the time because, although you can recognize the word when you see it or hear it, you can't naturally recall the word when you want to.

The only way for new words to truly become part of your vocabulary is to speak them repeatedly, putting them into real sentences that have real meaning. Eventually, the word will become a force of habit so that you can say it without even thinking.

Grammar

Let's say your friend asks you what you did yesterday, and you want to respond in Spanish:

What is "To walk" in Spanish?
"caminar"

Ok, time to use past tense, but should I use preterit or imperfect?
Preterit because you're talking about a single point in time.

What is the conjugation for "caminar" for the first person?
"caminé"

Your answer: "Ayer, caminé a la playa."

You may have studied all the grammar, but you would probably spend a good ten seconds thinking about this if you're not used to using grammar in conversations.

Speaking is the only thing that trains your brain and speeds up this thought process until you can respond in 1/10th of a second.

Listening

For many beginners, understanding native speakers is the number one challenge when learning Ukrainian or any other language.

When you are having a conversation with someone, you are speaking and training your ears at the same time. You are listening "actively," which means you are listening with the intent to respond. This forces you into a higher state of concentration, as opposed to "passively" listening to Ukrainian radio, for example, where you are simply taking in information.

Listening and speaking really go hand in hand.

Pronunciation

The first part of pronunciation is to understand how to correctly produce the sounds, which can be tricky, once you can do it right, the next part is about getting enough reps and saying the words out loud again and again.

Maybe at first, the words will make your tongue and lips feel strange, but over time, they will become part of your muscle memory until eventually it feels completely natural to say them.

When you learn a foreign language, you might find that it has some difficult sounds that you are not used to making. Fortunately, Ukrainian is a relatively easy language to pronounce. While there might be a few hard sounds, the vast majority of them are found in the English language.

To further help you, Ukrainian pronunciation mirrors the intonation patterns we're accustomed to in English. What this all boils down to is that if you're learning to speak Ukrainian, you will have an easier time than you might with some other languages.

When you begin to study Ukrainian pronunciation, you should start with the alphabet. After all, when you first learned the mechanics and written form of English, you started with the alphabet!

How to master the very tricky rules of Ukrainian pronunciation

You already know that Ukrainian isn't the easiest language to learn, but there is a big advantage you should know about: Ukrainian and English are both Indo-European languages so they have a lot in common. And they both have a pronunciation that's quite different from the written language. I can assure you the pronunciation is *not what you'd expect*— but with a few rules in mind, you'll be able to master the most common aspects of Ukrainian pronunciation!

Here are a few tips for improving your pronunciation:

1. Work on your pronunciation

This may seem obvious, but phonetics is very important for second language learners. You may know a lot of Ukrainian words, but if you are pronouncing them wrong you will be misunderstood by others. Just recall how difficult it is to listen to a person who ignores English language phonetic rules.

Communicate with native speakers as much as possible, listen to podcasts, music, and watch YouTube channels or TV in Ukrainian. Repeat after speakers. Remember: only practice makes perfect, nothing else.

2. Use exclamations and strengthening words

Exclamations are used a lot in the Ukrainian language. They emphasize emotions and attitudes. To sound more natural, you need to use them in your speech.

Some examples of emotional exclamations:

"ой" (like "oops"), "овва" (shows your surprise), "отакої" (expresses negative surprise), "агов" (like "hey"), long "ааа" (you just remembered or realized something), "ex/ox" (shows regret), etc.

3. Use diminutive forms of Ukrainian words

In Ukrainian, diminutives are used a lot. Many nouns and nearly all personal names have diminutive forms. Usually, the diminutive form of a word is formed by using diminutive suffixes: -ик, -ичка, -инка, -ина, -иця, -ок, -очка etc.

For example: кіт – котик (a cat – a kitten), собака – собачка (a dog – a puppy), квітка -квіточка (a flower – a small flower).

Names: Софія – Софіїчка, Марина – Маринка, Тетяна – Тетяночка.

4. Be aware of local dialects

To feel more confident as a speaker you need to know the "real language" of a place you are living in. The Ukrainian language is very diverse and people speak differently in every region.

For example, if you are planning to stay in the Lviv region, you need to know what "кобіта" (a woman, a girl), "канапка" (a sandwich) or "кнайпа" (a bar, a restaurant) mean.

5. Recognize slang words, and jargon of different social groups

All over the Ukraine, you will probably hear some youth slang words like: "жесть" (trash, hardcore), "капець" (end, trouble, breakdown), and "блін" (damn). These words come from Russian youth slang.

Of course, I don't recommend you to use slang words a lot, but at least you need to understand their meaning because being with locals you will hear them a lot.

Some of the most common mistakes for foreign speakers learning Ukrainian:

1. **ий** ending

This ending is used in the masculine gender adjectives: гáрний (nice, handsome), щасли́вий (happy), весéлий (joyful). **Ий** is pronounced as /yi/, but foreigners often make the mistake of saying /y/: гарни, щасливи, весели.

The sound **и** is also unique in its pronunciation. Think about **и** as the sound between **i** and **y.** If you say i and slowly try to pronounce y just after it, you'll hear и somewhere in between.

- Г and Х

Г is the voiced *glottal fricative* (ɦ in IPA). In phonetics it is *breathy voiced or murmured*, which means the vocal cords are loosely vibrating.

E.g.: гáрний (nice), гу́би (lips), готувáти (to cook).

You can listen to the sound on Wilipedia: (https://en.wikipedia.org/wiki/Voiced_glottal_fricative)

X is the voiceless *velar fricative*. The sound is produced by constricting air flow through a narrow channel at the place of articulation, causing turbulence. It is articulated with the back of the tongue at the soft palate.

The pronunciation of the Ukrainian x is similar to the pronunciation of ch in *loch* and *broch*.

E.g.: хло́пець (boy), холо́дний (cold), ходи́ти (walk).

You can listen to the sound on Wilipedia: (https://en.wikipedia.org/wiki/Voiceless_velar_fricative)

Common grammar mistakes:

- **Сього́дні 25 градуси.**

It's 25 degrees today.

Using numbers together with nouns, don't forget about the formula:

1 + N.c., sing. (1 (оди́н) гра́дус)

2,3,4 + N.c., plural (3 (три) гра́дуси)

5 + G.c., plural (6 (шість) гра́дусів)

The declension of nouns after numbers in the single digits depends on the last number.

E.g.: 31 (три́дцять оди́н) гра́дус

33 (три́дцять три) гра́дуси

37 (три́дцять сім) гра́дусів

Feminine gender nouns:

1 (одна́) годи́на

2 (дві) годи́ни

7 (сім) годи́н

Neutral gender nouns:

1 (одне́) вікно́

2 (два) вікна́

7 (сім) ві́кон

Remember: Numbers 1 and 2 have their gender variants.

E.g.: оди́н кіт, одна́ кі́шка; два коти́, дві кі́шки; одне́ вікно́, два вікна́.

Вчо́ра було́ 27 гра́дусів, а сього́дні 31 гра́дус.

Lexical mistakes

- **Question words звідки, куди і де**

Sometimes language-learners will say something like:

Де ти приїхав? (meaning: "Where did you come from?") Or
Де ти йдеш? (meaning: "Where do you go?")

Which is wrong. Take a look at these question words:

Звідки – where...from; how

E.g. Звідки ти? Where are you from?

Звідки ти знаєш? How do you know?

Куди – where to; which way

We use куди when we want to know a direction.

E.g. Куди ти йдеш? Where do you go?

Йому немає куди йти. There is nowhere he can go.

Де – where

Де ти живеш? Where do you live?

Де ти зараз? Where are you now?

- **Це хо́лодно сього́дні.**

The litteral translation of English "**it's**" doesn't work in Ukrainian.

So remember: don't use **це** (it) when discussing the weather or condition in locations.

У Каліфо́рнії завжди́ жа́рко. It's always hot in California.

У вас вдо́ма ча́сто ду́же чи́сто. It's often very clean in your home.

- **Я люблю́ мою кі́шку.**

I love my cat.

You might be surprised that the sentence above isn't correct.

This is because in Ukrainian it's not correct to use **я/мій, ти/твій, вона/її він/ його** etc. both in the same sentence.

Instead of the possessive pronoun you should use the reflexive possessive pronoun **свій**.

Я люблю́ свою́ кі́шку. I love my cat.

Він лю́бить **свого́** соба́ку. He loves his dog.

Вони́ лю́блять **свої́х** твари́н. They love their animals.

- **Передава́й "приві́т" Макси́му з Оле́ни.**

Say "hello" to Maksym from Olena.

It's very easy to confuse the usage of the preposition **з**.

The Ukrainian prepositions **з** and **від** in English are translated as **from**.

But in Ukrainian, they are used in different situations:

З before the location: Він **з** Аме́рики (Gen.C.). He is from America.

Я йду **з** магази́ну (Gen.C.). I'm leaving the store.

Від before animated nouns:

У ме́не є подару́нок **від** сестри́. I have a present from my sister.

Я йду додо́му **від** по́други. I'm going home from a friend's.

- **Я подо́бається ї́сти моро́зиво.**

I like to eat ice cream.

If you want to say that you like something, you should use the formula:

Dat.C. of a noun, pronoun+подобається (sing.)/подобаються (pl.)+ object (N.C.)

E.g.: Мені подобається цей пес. I like this dog.

Данилу подобаються маленькі машини. Danylo likes small cars.

- **Вечір / вчора**

These words are easy to confuse. **Вечір** – evening, **вчора** – yesterday.

Вчора був прекрасний **вечір**. Yesterday was a beautiful evening.

- **Чотири/чорний**

Another easy to confuse couple.

Чотири – four, **чорний** – black.

Я бачу чотири чорні чашки. I see four black cups.

Why correct pronunciation is so important

Proper pronunciation is important, very important. Some say it's even more important than getting the grammar perfectly correct! Why would this be?

Understanding

If communicating with native speakers matters to you when learning Ukrainian, you need to be understood when you talk, and you need to be able to understand the native speakers. After all, without understanding, the purpose of language is null and void!

In order to be understood, you need to be able to speak the language in a way that is familiar to native speakers, or at least recognizable by them.

When learning to speak a new language, you will learn that the more you progress the more intricate it becomes!

For instance, almost every language has vocabulary that may look the same in writing, but because the words are pronounced differently, they have very different meanings.

This means that you may say a word in Ukrainian, and because of a slight change in pronunciation, the meaning of the word changes completely. Understandably, this can make for pretty embarrassing situations! At worst, your mispronounced Ukrainian will sound garbled to a native speaker.

Knowing the nuances of how a word or letter is pronounced will also help you to understand spoken Ukrainian better.

Good communication

Not pronouncing Ukrainian or any other language correctly can lead to a lot of frustration because you're unable to express what you mean, and you will not be understood correctly.

Even if you have total knowledge of Ukrainian grammar, and can write it like a native, not knowing how to speak it properly will only make for very frustrating communication all around.

A good impression

Even if you're only a beginner, it is possible to speak any language correctly. This way, you are bound to make a good impression on native speakers, and when you're more fluent, you will be likely to garner a lot more respect than a fumbling newbie speaker who doesn't care much for correct pronunciation.

People often have a lot of patience for someone who learns to speak a new language, but native speakers are more likely to address you and engage with you in conversation if you work hard on your accent. This is simply because you'll be able to understand one another!

So, proficiency in pronunciation can mean the difference between having none or plenty of Ukrainian speaking friends. It will also serve you well in the workplace, and make you popular with your Ukrainian speaking managers and employers or employees.

Learning to speak Ukrainian properly is also a sign of respect for not only the language, but also the native speakers and their customs.

Secrets to learning correct pronunciation

Use voice recording tools to perfect your pronunciation. Watch and listen to Ukrainian speakers over and over again to train your ear, and watch their mouths as they speak. Then, copy the speech as best you can. Later, you can record yourself to hear if you sound like a native speaker and compare yourself with native speakers. It's great for self-motivation.

Practice in front of a mirror and check you're copying the correct lip and mouth movements.

Use an online dictionary

Look up words online and listen to the audio pronunciation. This will go a long way towards giving you an idea of how to pronounce a word or letter correctly.

Train your ear to the language

I know I have said this before but at the risk of repeating myself, make an effort to listen to Ukrainian music and recorded books, and watch plenty of Ukrainian movies and/or TV shows in Ukrainian. This will train your ear to the language, and you'll be surprised how quickly you pick up the accent. Remember, this is the way we learned to speak when we were young—mostly by listening to the adults talking, and repeating what they say.

Practice, practice, practice...

Repetition of the same thing may be boring, but in learning a new language, you're creating new pathways in your brain (this is also called neurolinguistics). For these to remain and become habitual, you will need to repeat the correct pronunciation often.

Make friends with a native Ukrainian speaker

Don't be shy to address them in Ukrainian! Ask them to correct you when you make a pronunciation mistake—this is a wonderful way to practice and learn the language first-hand, and also to make new friends.

Reading and writing

If you can say something in Ukrainian, then you'll have no problem reading and writing it as well.

However, the opposite isn't true. If you focus on reading and writing, it will not enable you to speak better.

Why?

Because, when you're speaking, everything happens in **seconds**, whereas reading and writing happen in **minutes**.

Only speaking will train your brain to think fast enough to keep up with conversations

80/20 your Ukrainian

Also called Pareto's principle, the 80/20 rule states that 80% of your results come from just 20% of your efforts.

This principle is absolutely huge when it comes to the best way to learn Ukrainian, and it has two major applications:

Vocabulary and grammar

The Ukrainian language is estimated to be made out of a total of 120,000 headwords, whereas the corpus it's built upon contains about 256,000. That's a lot of words!

- The 300 most common words make up 65% of spoken dialogue
- The 1,000 most common words make up 88% of spoken dialogue

So, as you can see, you don't NEED to learn every single last word. Start by focusing on the most common words and the words that are personally going to be useful to you based on your interests and goals.

Just like vocabulary, you want to focus on the most common grammar rules and conjugations (ex. present, preterit, future, conditional, etc.). There are lots of advanced grammar rules that aren't used very often in everyday speech, so they are simply less of a priority.

Learning methods

It seems like there are a million ways to learn Ukrainian these days, from traditional methods, like textbooks, to endless online resources. This creates a big problem for language learners: a lack of focus. A lot of people try to dabble in as many as five or six different learning methods and end up spreading themselves too thin.

Instead, **choose the one or two methods that are most effective (giving you 80% of the results)** and ignore the rest. Let's start by outlining some of the methods you could choose for your Ukrainian learning.

Popular learning methods

Which methods work, and which ones should you not bother with? Here is a subjective low down.

The reasons why 99% of software and apps won't make you fluent

Take a second and think of all the people you know who learned Ukrainian or any second language.

Did any of them become fluent by learning from an app?

Packed with fancy features, there are hundreds of apps and software out there that claim to be the ultimate, game-changing solution to help you learn a language.

- "Advanced speech recognition system!"
- "Adaptive learning algorithm..."
- "Designed by German scientists."
- "Teaches you a language in just three weeks!"

But do they really work? Is an app really the best way to learn Ukrainian?

Or should you file this stuff under the same category as the "Lose 30 pounds in 30 days" diet?

The biggest software and app companies, like Rosetta Stone, Babbel, Busuu, and Duolingo, have all funded their own "independent" studies on the effectiveness of their software. In other words, they all paid the same researcher, who came to the conclusion that every single one of the apps was the best thing since sliced bread.

For example, the study for Babbel concluded:
"...Users need on average 21 hours of study in a two-month period to cover the requirements for one college semester of Ukrainian."

This is no surprise because the fill-in-the-blanks, multiple-choice, one-word-at-a-time approach of software is the same kind of stuff you would find on a Ukrainian midterm in college.

The problem is that just like software, college and high school Ukrainian courses are notorious for teaching students a few basics while leaving them completely unable to actually speak.

At the end of the day, software and apps, just like the traditional courses you take in school, are missing a key ingredient: speaking with real people.

The best and fastest way to learn Ukrainian is to spend as much time as possible having real conversations. It's the way that languages have been learned for thousands of years, and although technology can help make this more convenient, it cannot be replaced.

Software companies like Rosetta Stone have finally realized this, and in recent years, they've tried to incorporate some sort of speaking element into their product.

The verdict? Their top review on Amazon was one out of five stars.

Ouch! But if software and apps can't really teach you to speak a language, then why are they so popular?

Because they've turned language learning into a game. Every time you get an answer right, there's a little "beep" that tells you that you did a great job, and soon enough, you are showered with badges, achievements, and cute little cartoons that make it feel like you're really getting it. Of course, these things are also used to guilt you into continuing to use their app. If you stop using them, they start sending you pictures of sad cartoon characters telling you they will die because of your lack of commitment. Really? Do they think we've all turned into four-year-olds?

In the real world, playing this game shields you from the difficult parts of learning a language. You can hide in your room, stare at your phone, and avoid the nervousness that comes with speaking Ukrainian in front of a native speaker or the awkward moment when you forget what to say.

But the reality is, every beginner who wants to learn Ukrainian will have to face these challenges sooner or later.

The 1% of apps that are actually useful
Despite the drawbacks of software and apps, there is one type of app that can have a profound impact on your learning, and we have been here before:

Electronic flashcards (also known as SRS, or "spaced repetition systems").

I know I have already been over this, but they really do work. Ok, I know they don't sound very glamorous, and maybe the last time you saw a flashcard was in the hands of that nerdy kid in fifth grade that who nobody wanted to sit with at lunchtime.

But please, bear with me because this can totally change the way you learn Ukrainian. Here's how a flashcard system works on an app.

Each flashcard will show you an English word, and you have to try and recall the Ukrainian word. If you get it wrong, it will show you the card again in one minute, but if you get it right, it will be a longer interval, like 10 minutes or a few days.

A typical basic flashcard app is Anki. (https://apps.ankiweb.net).

Flashcard apps work by repeatedly forcing you to recall words that you struggle to remember, and as you get better, the word shows up less and less frequently. As soon as you feel like you're going to forget a new word, the flashcard will pop up and refresh it.

This system helps you form very strong memories and will allow you to manage a database of all the words you've learned, even those you picked up months or years ago.

You can also use flashcards for grammar concepts. For example, if you're having trouble remembering the conjugations for verbs, just make each conjugation a separate flashcard.

By putting all your conjugations in all the different tenses into flashcards, you now have a way to repeatedly drill them into your memory.

The major advantage of flashcards is that all you really need is 10-20 minutes a day. Every single day, we spend a lot of time waiting around, whether it's for public transportation, in line at the supermarket, or for a doctor's appointment. This is all wasted time that you can use to improve your vocabulary. It only takes a few seconds to turn on the flashcard app and review a few words.

If you want to try this out, these are probably the two best apps out there:

Anki (https://apps.ankiweb.net)
The original, "pure" flashcard app.

Pros:
- Reviewing cards is extremely simple and straightforward.
- Very easy to write your own cards; it can be done on the fly.
- Plenty of customization options and user-written decks to download (although not as many as Memrise).

Cons:
- It can be a bit confusing to set up; you need to be tech-savvy.
- It doesn't provide reminders/motivation to practice daily.

Cost:
- Free for Android, computer.
- US$24.99 for iOS. (At time of writing)

Memrise (https://www.memrise.com)

Flashcard-based app with modern features.

Pros:

- More variety for reviewing cards (fill-in-the-blanks, audio recordings, etc.).
- Offers a little bit of gamification (rewards, reminders) to keep you motivated.
- It has a big library of card decks written by other people and a large community of users.

Cons:

- Writing your own cards (called "Create a Course") is not as easy as Anki and can't be done on mobile.
- The review system works differently from traditional cards.

Cost:

- Free for all platforms (iOS, Android, computer).

Both apps come with standard Ukrainian vocabulary decks as well as those written by other users. However, the real beauty of flashcards is being able to write the decks yourself. There is a big advantage to doing this, which you can see from the following steps:

When using pre-written flashcards

- You see a new word for the first time in your app and then review the word until you remember it.

When making flashcards yourself

- You get exposed to a new world through conversation, your teacher, or something you've seen or heard. You associate the word with a real-life situation.
- You write it into a flashcard, and by doing this, you're already strengthening your memory of that word.
- You review the word until you remember it.

As you can see, while making the cards yourself takes a bit of extra work, you get to control the words you learn and can focus on the ones that are more meaningful to you. Plus, the process of writing the word down acts as an extra round of review.

While it is true that flashcard apps have a bit of a learning curve, they are very easy once you get the hang of them, and you'll notice a huge difference in memorizing vocabulary and grammar.

Can you learn Ukrainian by just watching TV and listening to the radio?

Countless beginners have tried and failed to learn Ukrainian by what is known as "passive listening." Examples of passive listening include:

- Audio courses
- Radio and podcasts
- Movies and TV shows

The idea of passive listening sounds good on paper. You can learn Ukrainian by listening to an audio course in your car on the way to work. Put on some Ukrainian radio while you're making dinner and then sit down for an episode of *Servant of the People* while you fold your laundry.

Except this doesn't work. Why?

Because learning a language is an ACTIVE process. You can't spend hundreds of hours listening to stuff in the background and expect your brain to figure it all out.

Now, many people will have a couple of objections to this:

I thought passive listening is how babies learn languages?

Let's assume out of simplicity that a baby is awake for an average of eight hours a day for the first year of its life. Through all the feedings and diaper changes, it is constantly being exposed to language because its parents are talking to it (and each other). So, by the time a baby says their first words at around the one-year mark, it has already had about three thousand hours of passive-listening exposure (8 hours x 365 days).

Now, how do you compete with that as a busy adult? Even if you squeeze in an hour a day of Ukrainian radio into your daily life, it would still take you eight years to get the equivalent amount of language exposure. Who has the patience to spend eight years learning Ukrainian?

Don't sell yourself short. With the right method and motivation, you can learn the Ukrainian you need in months, not years.

If you incorporate a bit of Ukrainian into every aspect of your life, then that's immersion, right? Isn't immersion the best way to learn Ukrainian?

There are many expats who have lived in Spain or Latin America for 5-10 years, and guess what? They STILL can't speak a word of Spanish let alone form a sentence.

These people have the perfect environment to learn, they can hear Spanish everywhere when walking down the street, and every friend or acquaintance is someone they can practice with. But somehow, none of this seems to help.

Why?
Because they don't make an effort to speak.

Immersion is extremely effective, but only if you take advantage of the environment you're in and speak Ukrainian every chance you get. Simply being there and listening is not enough.

As an adult, we have to learn languages actively. Most of us want to go from beginner to fluent in as short a time as possible, and passive listening is simply too slow.

If you're already listening to a lot of Ukrainian, it doesn't mean you should stop. Try to do it actively, which means giving it 100% of your attention rather than having it in the background as you're doing something else.

Listening to radio, TV, and movies can be useful at a later stage. Increasing the amount of Ukrainian you hear will speed up your progress when you are already at a conversational level.

But when it comes to learning Ukrainian as a complete beginner, there are far more efficient methods.

How to practice Ukrainian

We've already established that the best way to learn Ukrainian for beginners involves speaking as much as possible. Let's go over the four main ways that you practice speaking Ukrainian:

Speak with people you know

Maybe you have friends who are native Ukrainian speakers, or maybe you are dating or married to one! If that person is the reason you wanted to learn Ukrainian in the first place, it may seem like a good idea to practice with them from the beginning.

Pros:

- It's free.
- Practicing with people you know can be less intimidating than with a stranger, and as a result, you

might be more willing to open up and speak (although, for some people, it has the opposite effect).

- They know you, and they like you, so they will probably be very supportive and patient with you.

Cons:

- You may not know anyone in your immediate circle of friends and family who speak Ukrainian.
- When you make a mistake, they probably won't be able to explain what you did wrong. Most native speakers don't know the rules of their own language. Things "just sound right" to them.
- People have deeply ingrained habits. Once a relationship is established, it is really hard to change the language of communication. You can try to practice Ukrainian with your wife, who is a native speaker, but more often than not, you'll find yourselves defaulting back to English because "it's just easier."
- Trying to practice Ukrainian with friends and family can be frustrating. You're going to stutter, you won't be able to express yourself the way you usually do, and your wonderful sense of humor will suddenly become nonexistent. You'll feel guilty that you're being an inconvenience to them (although most of the time it's a bigger deal for you than it is for them).

Go to Meetups

Ukrainian learners often get together a few times a week at a public place (usually a café) and practice speaking for an hour or two. A good place to find them is Meetup.com (https://www.meetup.com). Just do a search for "Ukrainian + *the city you live in.*"

Pros:

- It's free.
- You get to meet new people in your area who are learning Ukrainian just like you. Since you're all in the same boat, you can encourage each other and help each other stay accountable.
- You can share learning tips with each other, like what's working and what's not.
- If you need an explanation for a grammar concept, chances are someone in the group knows and can explain it to you.

Cons:

- You'll only be able to find meetups in big cities. If you live in a smaller city or town, then you're out of luck.
- It's not great for shy people. Speaking in a group of 10-15 people can be pretty intimidating.
- What often happens at meetups is that you all sit around a table and two or three people will end up doing most of the talking (remember the 80/20 rule?) while the rest just sit there and listen.
- Everyone is at different levels of fluency, so you could find yourself talking to someone who is way

more advanced than you are, and you may end up boring them. Unfortunately, some groups don't let complete beginners join for this very reason.

- If you are just starting out and don't feel confident in speaking, you might end up doing a whole lot listening and not much talking. You get much better value out of meetups if you are already somewhat conversational.

Language exchanges

The basic idea is to find a native Ukrainian speaker who is trying to learn English. You meet in person or have a Skype call (or something similar) where you split your time practicing both Ukrainian and English. The easiest way to find a partner is through online exchanges like My Language Exchange (https://www.mylanguageexchange.com) and Conversation Exchange (https://www.conversationexchange.com).

Pros:

- It's free.
- You get exposure to a lot of different people who come from different backgrounds.

Cons:

- It can be very time consuming to find the right language partner. It can take a lot of trial and error.

- You only get to spend 50% of your time speaking in Ukrainian.
- Your partner won't be able to speak English well, so it can be tough to communicate if both of you are beginners.
- Your partner probably won't be able to explain Ukrainian grammar to you, and you won't be able to explain English very well, either. For example, can you explain when you should use "which" vs. "that"? Or how about "who" vs. "whom"?
- Partners can be flaky since there is no paid commitment, and some people simply don't show up at the agreed time (happens more often in online exchanges).

Professional Ukrainian teachers

These days it is far more convenient to find a Ukrainian teacher online, and believe it or not, this can be even more interactive than being face-to-face. You participate in your lessons via Skype from the comfort of home and on your own schedule. This is how many people prefer to learn Ukrainian.

Pros:

- A good teacher is like having your own coach or personal trainer. They want you to succeed, and they are there to support you and offer motivation and advice. It is much easier to learn Ukrainian when someone is there to hold you accountable.

- A teacher is a trained professional. They have comprehensive knowledge of both Ukrainian and English grammar, so they can explain to you the difference between the two, and provide a lot of useful examples to help you understand difficult concepts.
- Teachers know how to correct you when you make a mistake, but not so often as to interrupt the flow of conversation. Talking to a teacher just feels natural.
- Even if you're the shyest person in the world, a good teacher knows how to coax you into speaking and how to build your confidence. You don't have to worry about making mistakes, you'll no longer feel embarrassed, and ultimately, you'll have fun.
- A teacher can quickly figure out your strengths and weaknesses and come up with a learning plan to address them.
- They will design a customized curriculum for you based on your learning goals and interests. This ensures that whatever they teach will be very meaningful to you.
- A good Ukrainian teacher should provide you with all the materials that you'll need, so you won't have to buy a textbook or spend time looking for grammar exercises.
- While a good chunk of your time is spent having conversations, your teacher will introduce exercises that cover all language skills, including pronunciation, reading, writing, and listening.

Cons:

- Just like language exchange partners, it can take some trial and error to find the right teacher. This is true especially if you are looking through an online teacher directory that doesn't do a great job of screening their teachers. You can waste hours scrolling through teacher profiles (which all seem to have five star ratings), only to be disappointed with the one you chose.
- Teachers aren't free. But getting a private teacher is a lot more affordable than you think...

Sure, there are plenty of "high end" teachers who will try to charge you as much as US$60-80/hour. On the "low end," you can probably find someone for less than US$15/hour, although they are usually unqualified tutors who can barely explain things better than your average native speaker.

Verbalicity has a good offer of "high-end" teaching for as little as US$20/hour. You can try out the first lesson for free. Go to: https://verbalicity.com

Of course, there are plenty of people who have learned Ukrainian without a teacher. Doing a language exchange or going to a meetup is certainly better than not speaking at all, but it will take much longer to learn, and you may be tempted to give up in the process.

So, if you've got a busy schedule and want to learn Ukrainian fast, then getting a teacher is definitely the best way to go.

Road Map: Zero to Conversational

We've just isolated some of the key concepts and methods that make up the best ways to learn Ukrainian. Now let's go through the three stages of learning. For each stage, we'll recap what the main goals and recommended method of learning are and offer some more tips on how to progress as quickly as possible.

Stage 1: Introduction

This stage is for absolute beginners. If you already have some knowledge of Ukrainian or are used to hearing it, then you can skip to the next stage.

Objective:

The idea is to get a brief introduction to Ukrainian with the goal of familiarizing yourself with the following:

- What spoken Ukrainian sounds like.
- How it feels to pronounce Ukrainian words.
- A few basic phrases.

This helps you acclimatize to learning a new language and gets you used to listening and speaking right away.

After this stage, you probably will have some basic phrases under your belt, like "My name is…", "Where are you from?" and "What time is it?"

How to do it:

Start with a free audio course or one of the popular apps. Ideally, it should be a guided course that's easy to follow. Here are some examples:

- 17 Minute Languages audio course, Google Play: Learn Ukrainian Free.
- Get Memrise (https://www.memrise.com) and start using their basic Ukrainian course, or use other free apps like Duolingo (https://www.duolingo.com).

"Wait," you are no doubt be saying to yourself, "didn't he say that apps can't teach you a language?"

That's true. But I didn't say they couldn't help, and at this point in time, all you're trying to do is get your bearings and get comfortable with listening and repeating.

You probably only need about 30 minutes a day, and this introductory stage should last no more than a few weeks.

Afterward, you can cut down or stop using these resources altogether because, although they are fine as an introduction, they are slow and inefficient. You should move on to better options, which we'll cover next.

Tip for this stage:

Focus on pronunciation

Try to get your pronunciation right from the very beginning. When you hear the Ukrainian recording, make sure you repeat it out loud.

At first, repeat each word slowly, syllable by syllable, until you can mimic the sounds almost perfectly. If necessary, record yourself speaking and listen back.

Once you're satisfied that you're saying it right, then repeat it over and over again until it feels natural.

Stage 2: Beginner

Objective:

At this stage, the goal is to build a solid foundation for yourself in terms of basic grammar and vocabulary, put your thoughts into complete sentences, and be confident enough to talk to people.

At the end of this stage, you want to be able to have basic conversations that involve exchanging information, asking for things, and talking about work, family, and your interests.

Effectively, you want to be at an upper-beginner level.

How to do it:

For the beginner stage, the best way to learn Ukrainian is to choose one of these two options:

Option 1:

- Textbook
- Speaking practice: friends, meetups, exchanges, Skype.
- Flashcards (optional)

Using a textbook might seem old-fashioned, but it is still probably the best way for a beginner to learn the grammatical rules of Ukrainian. The reason why a textbook is effective is that it teaches you in a structured way. It takes you through a progression that slowly builds on each concept, step by step.

For each chapter of the textbook that you go through, study the dialogues and make sure you do all the practice exercises. Ideally, you should try to find additional exercises online related to the concept you just learned.

Just like most forms of learning, a textbook can't actually teach you to speak. So, for each concept you learn, you need to be practicing it with real people.

You can use a combination of friends, meetups, or language exchanges to get your practice in. At this point, you are not having full conversations yet (nor should you try to). Try practicing phrases and some short dialogues or scenarios. But nevertheless, you should aim for one to two hours per week of speaking practice.

Option 2:

- Learn with a Ukrainian teacher in person or online

- Flashcards (optional)

When you learn with a teacher, you get step-by-step guidance and speaking practice all in one package.
A good Ukrainian teacher will send or give you textbook materials and all the practice exercises you'll ever need, so there is no need to look for materials on your own. You even get homework, just like in school.

A teacher can also explain grammar to you in different ways and answer your questions if you don't understand. This is a big advantage over someone who is just studying on their own.

Being able to practice what you learned immediately through speaking is another advantage. For example, you might spend the first half of a lesson going over the conjugations of the Imperfect tense and then spend the second half the lesson practicing it verbally through question and answer, storytelling, and other fun exercises.

Flashcards

It is never too early to start using flashcards to help you remember words.

But especially if you've chosen Option 1, it might be a little overwhelming to be studying while trying to find practice opportunities, and you don't want to add another method like flashcards to distract you from that.

Remember the 80/20 rule. It is better to focus on a few things that have the highest impact.

But if you feel like you're having trouble remembering new words or grammar conjugations, then it's probably time to incorporate flashcards into your routine.

Tips for this stage:

Don't jump ahead

It might be tempting to immediately work your way through a textbook from cover to cover, but this will just overload you with information.

A lot of people make the mistake of diving too deep into the grammar without making sure that they fully understand and have practiced each concept before moving on to the next. If in doubt, spend more time reviewing what you've already learned.

Be strategic about your vocabulary

Focus on memorizing the most useful words that will make it easier for you to practice speaking. Highly useful words include "power verbs" and "connectors." You can find these online or in any decent text book

If you master these types of words, your speech will come out more naturally, and it will make you sound more fluent than you actually are at this point. This can give you a much-needed boost of confidence because, at this stage, it can still be scary to be out there talking to people.

Intermediate

Objective:

This stage is all about expanding your horizons. It's about greatly increasing your vocabulary, comprehension skills, and confidence in using Ukrainian in a variety of situations.

At the end of this stage, you want to be able to express yourself freely and talk about different topics, like what's happening in the news, your hopes and dreams, or your opinion on a particular subject.

You're still going to make plenty of mistakes, and your grammar won't be perfect, but the goal is to be able to get your ideas across, whatever they may be. If you can do that, you'll reach the upper intermediate level and be considered **conversationally fluent**.

Some may choose to improve their Ukrainian even further, to more advanced levels, but for many people, this is this level where you can fully enjoy the rewards of being able to speak Ukrainian.

How to do it:

Based on the two options from the beginner stage, we can make a few adjustments for the intermediate level:

Option 1:

- Speaking practice (*friends, meetups, exchanges*)
- Reading and listening
- Flashcards
- Textbooks (*optional*)

Option 2:

- Learn with a Ukrainian teacher
- Reading and listening
- Flashcards

Speaking practice

To move into the intermediate stage, speaking becomes even more important. By now you should be ramping up your speaking practice to a **minimum of two to three hours per week**.

Whereas you were previously practicing short phrases or dialogues, you should now be able to have more full-fledged conversations because you know more vocabulary and grammar.

If you are learning with a teacher, you should know them pretty well by now, so you can have deeper conversations about more diverse topics. Your teacher can also start to speak a little bit faster to help train your ear.

Active Reading/Listening

This is the stage where active reading and listening start to shine. You know enough Ukrainian now that you can really take advantage of movies, TV, radio, podcasts, books, and articles.

You won't understand 100% of what you read and hear. Heck, maybe you only understand 50-60% at this point, but that is enough to get the gist of what is going on. If you're watching TV shows or movies, turn on Ukrainian subtitles (Netflix is great for this). Reading and listening at the same time will get you the best results.

Try to find material that is interesting to you. This way, you can enjoy the process of listening and reading, which can become a source of motivation. You'll also pick up Ukrainian that is relevant and useful to you personally.

Remember, "Active" means giving it your full attention. Try your best to understand it and pay attention to the grammar and vocabulary and the context in which they are being used. If there is anything you don't understand, write it down so you can look it up later, or ask your teacher during your next lesson.

Flashcards

A big part of going from beginner to intermediate is significantly increasing your vocabulary. By now, you will have already learned all the "easy" words, and to further build your vocabulary, you need to be very deliberate about remembering all the new words you are exposed to every day. Using flashcard apps like Anki or Memrise can really help commit them to memory. You can practice in five-minute chunks (while waiting for the bus, etc.) for a total of 10-20 minutes a day to get great results.

Textbook

A textbook is not mandatory at this point. You've learned most of the important grammar, and now the focus should be to practice it until you can use it fluidly.

Of course, there are always more advanced grammar concepts to learn, but they tend to be used very sparingly in everyday conversations.

Tips for this stage:

Learning formula

Your "routine" for learning new material should look something like this:

- You're exposed to new Ukrainian vocabulary and grammar through your teacher and textbook or by listening and reading.
- Review it using flashcards.
- Speak it until it becomes second nature.

For example, you hear a phrase on a Ukrainian TV show which you are not familiar with.

You look up the meaning and then create a new flashcard in Anki.

The next day, the flashcard pops up, and you review it.

A few days later, you head to your Ukrainian meetup, and during a conversation bring up the phrase

Staying Motivated

When you reach the intermediate stage, you may feel like you're not progressing as fast as you did before. In fact, there will be times where you feel like you aren't improving at all.

This is the classic "dip" that comes with learning any skill, and Ukrainian is no exception.

This happens because you've already learned a lot of the "low-hanging fruit." What you are learning now is more incremental and takes longer for everything to click in your mind.

To overcome the dip, you need to trust the process and be disciplined when it comes to the learning formula.

Your teacher can really help you stay motivated by creating a plan that guides you to new things you should learn and older concepts you should be reviewing, as well as giving you feedback on what you are doing well and what you need to improve on.

Time Frame

So, how long does it take to learn Ukrainian using this road map?

I'm not going to lie to you and say that you can become fluent in 30 days. Maybe some people can, but most of us lead busy lives, with jobs, families, and other responsibilities competing for our time.

If you are learning with a Ukrainian teacher (Option 2), I believe that you can go from zero to conversationally fluent in **8–12 months** using the methods in this road map.

This assumes that you can spend **one hour per day** working on your Ukrainian, whether that's the actual Ukrainian lessons themselves, reviewing flashcards, or actively listening and reading.

This timeframe is just an estimate because, obviously, everyone learns at a different pace. Of course, the more time you dedicate to learning Ukrainian, the faster you'll progress.

If you decide to go at it alone (Option 1), it will take a lot longer. But if you follow the best way to learn Ukrainian as outlined in the road map, stay disciplined, and make sure you consistently get enough conversation practice, you'll get there eventually.

Final Thoughts

Absolutely anyone can learn Ukrainian.

It doesn't matter whether or not you have a talent for languages or whether you are a naturally fast learner.

At the end of the day, learning Ukrainian is about motivation, focus, and time.

If you've got all three of these things and you commit to speaking rather than just learning the "stuff" of Ukrainian, then you simply cannot fail.

And of course, don't forget to have FUN! The process should be as enjoyable as the end goal.

CHAPTER FIFTEEN

LEARNING WITHOUT TRYING

Remember the story about the lazy bricklayer way back in Chapter One? Well, to recap, the lazy way, or the way that involves the least amount of work, is most often the smartest way to do things.

Do the things that involve the least amount of work when learning a language. Engage in effortless language learning, not completely effortless, of course, but as effortless as possible.

The word "effortless" in this context is borrowed from two sources. One is AJ Hoge, who is a great teacher of English. His channel and website are both called Effortless English. The other source is Taoist philosophy.

Effortlessness and the Parable of the Crooked Tree

When the linguist Steve Kaufmann (who, incidentally, can speak over 20 languages) wrote his book *The Linguist: A Personal Guide to Language Learning*, he began with what he called "The Parable of the Crooked Tree."

The author of the parable was Zhuangzi, an early exponent of Taoism, a school of Chinese philosophy from over two thousand years ago. Zhuangzi's basic principle in life was to follow what was natural, what was effortless, and not try to force things.

Typically, the Taoist philosophy was in opposition to Confucianism, which prescribed rules of what you should and shouldn't do to be a great person. Confucianism is full of admonishments on how you should behave. As is often the case with prescriptive philosophies or religions, these "commandments" attempt to set the boundaries of correct behavior. Zhuangzi was different. He advised people to follow their own natures and to not resist the world around them. This effortless non-resistance would help them learn better and be happier.

In Zhuangzi's parable of the crooked tree, his friend Huizi tells him that a tree they are both observing is crooked because the lumber is not good for anything, like Zhuangzi's philosophy.

"Neither your philosophy nor the tree is good for anything," says Huizi.

Zhuangzi replies, "You say that because you don't know how to use them. You have to use things for the purpose intended and understand their true nature. You can sit underneath a crooked tree and enjoy its shade, for example. If you understand the true nature of things, you will be able to use them to achieve your goals."

My extended Italian family are in the lumber business, and sometimes those gnarly old trees produce very expensive and decorative wood. Compared to trees in a planted forest, their wood is less uniform and less suitable for industrial end uses. We just have to accept these more individualistic trees as they are and appreciate what they bring. Zhuangzi defends his philosophy, saying it is useful if we accept its nature and know how to use it.

Zhuangi's philosophy was based on effortlessness, "wu wei" (无为) in Chinese. In other words, if you want to learn better, stop resisting; go with the flow. That has always been my approach. Language learning does require some effort, of course, but we learn best when effort is minimized and pleasure is maximized.

Let's look at something that requires effort but is also usually enjoyable: reading.

If you are reading in a language that you read well and you come across a few unknown words, you usually don't look up those unknown words in a dictionary because it's too much trouble and you have usually worked out the meaning because of the context.

So, what happens if you are reading something in Ukrainian as a beginner and have to constantly resort to dictionaries? They are no longer the learning aid they once were but become a chore and a block to enjoying reading in the way you are accustomed. And what's worse, if you don't memorize these new words' meanings, you will keep on getting bogged down. So, is there a better or easier way to start off reading in Ukrainian—an effortless way?

Thankfully, yes, there is. It is called LingQ (https://www.lingq.com/en/learn-ukrainian-online/) You can read in Ukrainian using LingQ on your computer, laptop, iPad, or smartphone.

When you look up a word in LingQ, it's highlighted. The word then appears highlighted in any subsequent material so you are reminded that you've looked it up before. You can see the meaning straight away, and eventually it becomes part of you, without any effort.

You are not just looking words up in a dictionary and then forgetting them. You are creating your own personal database of words and phrases for easy review as you continue reading.

Steve Kaufmann highly recommends this as a way of learning a language, and he should know. He has similar practical thoughts on grammar:

When I read grammar – and I believe we should occasionally read grammar rules as it helps give us a sense of the language – I don't try to remember anything.

I don't try to learn or understand anything. I just treat it as a spark, an exposure of something that might help me eventually get a sense of the language. I don't worry about grammar. I know it will gradually become clearer for me.

Have you ever noticed how some people can learn languages effortlessly (Steve Kaufmann would be one), getting to fluency faster with pen and paper than others do with a bag full of textbooks and phone-full of learning apps?

Everything about their learning seems effortless, and every new word and expression they learn is used with utmost confidence.

What is it about these individuals that sets them apart?

Every language learner strives for this effortlessly cool way of learning, where study ceases to be a chore and language usage becomes commonplace.

While it may seem like these individuals were born with a natural linguistic talent, it actually all comes down to a few simple habits these super-learners integrate into their daily life.

Here's a short list, along with some tips on implementing these habits in your daily life and becoming the confident speaker you want to be.

Note: You do not have to follow these recommendations exactly; adapt them to your lifestyle and unique personality.

Review before learning, even if it means you don't have time or energy to learn more.

Effective language learners know that what you don't review, you forget forever, and forgetting means that all that time you've spent learning the new word or expression has been put to waste.

That is why you should always prioritize reviewing above learning and start every study session by going over your past notes and flashcards.

That way, if you realize halfway through that you're just too exhausted to make the progress you hoped for, you've at least made sure you don't regress by activating all the connections already in your brain!

Tip: Never learn something new before you review what you know already.

Study a little bit every day and don't mistake the illusion of progress for actual improvement.

Effective language learners understand that binge-learning is but an illusion of progress.

When you try to learn long lists of vocabulary all at once or leaf through a textbook, chapter after chapter, without giving the necessary thought to the information within, your brain starts a tally that addictively goes up with every leaf.

The problem is, that mental counter represents the number of words and lessons you've seen, not the information you can actually use, or even remember the next morning.

Binge learning is extremely motivating at the beginning, but it consistently leads to burnout when the rational part of your brain finally realizes that all this euphoria was, in fact, unjustified.

Tip: Study in small chunks every day, even if for just five or 10 minutes.

Have a clear goal and use the language for something you already enjoy.

Effective learners realize that you can't learn a language without motivation that comes from the prospect of using it in the context you're passionate about.

For example: If you love horses, include equestrian themes throughout your learning. If you enjoy scuba diving like me, include Ukrainian-speaking scuba-diving sites in your learning.

Tip: Use the language in the context of the topics you're passionate about and the activities you enjoy.

Avoid having a closet full of unopened textbooks or a phone full of learning apps.

Effective language learners know that there's no silver bullet to language learning, so they don't waste time searching for it. They choose an effective method quickly and stick to it until there is a real need to change.

One mistake beginners in language learning fall victim to again and again is going on a shopping spree for learning resources only to realize that they are spending more time scavenging for new ways to learn than actually learning.

It's good to choose a methodology that works for you, but it's even more important to do so quickly and get back to learning.

Tip: Spend a week researching different learning methods, select one or two that suit you best, and stick with them until you've read them cover to cover or identify a clear need to supplement them with another resource.

Strike a balance between consuming the language and using it to convey your thoughts.

Effective learners value output as much as input and make sure to write or say a new word out loud every time they read or listen to one.

There are countless examples of language learners who spend all their time cramming vocabulary only to find themselves at a loss for words when thrown into a real-life conversation.

There are also countless examples of those who dedicate every minute to speaking to friends and blogging in the target language. Such students are often remarkably fluent in their specific topic of interest or when they speak to their usual interlocutors, but they can struggle to produce a single coherent sentence outside of that context.

No matter your ultimate goal, it is crucial to learn languages in a balanced way. Reading and listening to native material on a diverse range of topics will enrich your own expressiveness. Using new words and expressions you've picked up from others will cement them in your memory.

Tip: Dedicate as much time to speaking and writing as to reading and listening and try to regularly wander into topics outside your comfort zone.

You will often fail, so celebrate your mistakes as opportunities to get better.

Effective learners value mistakes and misunderstandings as opportunities to learn and improve.

Everyone remembers Henry Ford's Model T, but what preceded it was a very imperfect Model A. Ford's mechanics gathered real-world insight into all its deficiencies and fixed them one at a time before coming up with the icon of the automotive history.

The only way to improve is to start using new expressions right after you learn them, make mistakes, and use those mistakes to improve your abilities.

It's not a failure to use the wrong grammar or make a blatant spelling mistake. The only true failure is when you don't learn from the mess-up or use it as an excuse to give up.

Tip: Don't look at mistakes as failures but rather as immediate opportunities to improve your language abilities.

Always be attentive and try to imitate the way native speakers use the language.

Effective learners mimic what expressions native speakers use in a given context, how they pronounce them, and what gestures they choose to reinforce their message.

Textbooks and dictionaries are great at teaching you what's grammatically correct, but they can't guide you to speak naturally in day-to-day situations. An expression that would give you full marks on a test, and pass every spell check, may sound absolutely jarring in the real world.

The best way to learn the language as it is actually spoken is to put yourself in context with native speakers and listen carefully to what they say! Then note down the natural sentence patterns you hear and use them yourself.

Next time you're queuing up for a matcha latte, stop trying to imagine the conversation you'll have with the barista and instead listen to the conversations she's having with other clients!

Tip: Always be attentive to what native speakers say in any given situation and note down the sentence patterns they use.

Let's leave this chapter by just recapping some of the major points made throughout this book:

- Something inside you has got to want to learn the language.
- Ignore grammar at the beginning and concentrate instead on learning new words.
- Work on learning the most commonly used words and forget about words that are rarely ever used.
- Make language learning automatic by listening, reading, and digesting the language wherever you can.
- And finally, find ways to make learning fun by reading new books, subscribing to blogs, translating street signs, listening to music, or conversing with strangers.

I leave you with the immortal words of Fatboy Slim: *"Just lay back and let the big beat lead you."*

CONCLUSION

If you have learned one thing from this book, I hope it is that the most effective learning is not obtained by trying too hard. If you fill your head with useless vocabulary and grammar rules you do not need to speak Ukrainian, eventually you will burn out and give up. Just keep to the bare minimum when starting out, find what works for you, and stick with that until something more effective comes your way.

You will have gathered by now that learning to speak Ukrainian is different from just learning Ukrainian. The emphasis is always on speaking. and understanding.

Learn at your own pace; do not force it. Find your own way. It is better to go slowly but surely rather than rush. The tortoise will always do better than the hare in language learning.

My abiding hope is that by the end of this book, you will have found your own path to speaking Ukrainian fluently and effortlessly.

Щасти!

BIBLIOGRAPHY / ONLINE RESOURCES

I have literally begged, borrowed, or stolen a lot of the content of this book, and I am indebted to the authors, teachers, website owners, app writers, and bloggers who have spent valuable time putting resources online or in print to help people learn a new language. I will list them after this brief epilogue.

I urge you to use the resources they have made available. Find what works for you. It may be a combination of all or some of them, or even just one. If you can't afford to buy their stuff, use the free stuff until you can. It will be well worth it.

By the way, I do not receive any sort of commission or kickback for recommending any of the courses, websites, blogs, or apps mentioned throughout this book. The fact that I have included them is based purely on merit. Any of these *helpers* will stand you in good stead.

I was lucky. I started learning new languages when I was young, sometimes out of necessity (just to be understood by my peers) and sometimes out of precocious curiosity. As an adult I got a degree in International Communication and became a linguist. I worked most of my life as an interpreter and translator.

I was also - and still am - filled with wanderlust and spent my mid- and late-teenage years hitchhiking around Europe (without a penny to my name and devoid of any dictionary, travel guide, or even map). "Ah," I hear you say, "that's why it was so easy for you, but I'm an adult, and I have a million things on my mind and a trillion things to do. It's so easy when you are a kid. You don't have to worry about anything else apart from living. I have so many responsibilities."

Yes and no. Kids do worry about a spectacular amount of things, and a lot of their time is tied up with doing things they also consider important.

What makes the difference with learning like a child is that children learn or assimilate a language faster because, one, they have fewer hang-ups about making mistakes and interacting with other language speakers, and two, they learn better when they are having fun and are interested. This is when they are seemingly picking up the language effortlessly.

My aim is to rekindle some of that emotion in you. Stick your thumb in the air, hitch a lift from whatever resource gets you moving, sit back, and enjoy the ride. Make this journey fun and exciting, and you will speak Ukrainian at the end of it.

- Anki (https://apps.ankiweb.net/) SRS (spaced repetition software) with intelligent flashcards.
- CoffeeBreak Languages (https://coffeebreaklanguages.com/category/one-minute-ukrainian/) Learn Ukrainian on your coffee break.

- ConversationExchange (https://www.conversationexchange.com) Practice with native speakers in your area.
- Duolingo (https://www.duolingo.com/) Fun podcast for learning Ukrainian.
- Експрес (https://expres.online/) Online Ukrainian newspaper.
- FluentU (https://www.fluentu.com/en/) SRS app and language immersion online.
- Free 101 Ukrainian (https://www.101languages.net/ukrainian/) Free Ukrainian lessons for beginners.
- italki (https://www.italki.com/) Online teaching and conversation resource.
- Languages-Direct (https://www.languages-direct.com/) Ukrainian printed and audio materials audio magazine.
- LingQ (https://www.lingq.com/en/) Online reading resource.
- Meetup (https://www.meetup.com/) Online language exchange.
- Memrise (https://www.memrise.com/) Memory techniques to speed up language learning.
- My Language Exchange (mylanguageexchange.com) Online language exchange community.
- SuperMemo (https://www.supermemo.com/en) SRS app.
- The Positivity Blog (https://www.positivityblog.com/) Henrik Edberg's positivity blog.
- Ukrainian recipes (https://ukrainian-recipes.com/history-of-ukrainian-cuisine)

- Verbalicity (https://verbalicity.com/) One-on-one online lessons with native teachers.

Printed in Great Britain
by Amazon

12390830R00190